Men of the LNER

'Steam Past' Books from Allen & Unwin

Men of the LNER

Peter Grafton

London
GEORGE ALLEN & UNWIN
Boston   Sydney

First published in 1982

GEORGE ALLEN & UNWIN LTD
40 Museum Street, London WC1A 1LU

British Library Cataloguing in Publication Data

Grafton, Peter
    Men of the LNER.
    1. London and North Eastern Railway – History
    2. Railroads – Great Britain – Employees –
    Biography
    I. Title
    385′.0941   HG3020.L8

    ISBN 0–04–385085–5

Picture research by Mike Esau

Set in 10/12 point Bembo by Nene Phototypesetters Ltd
and printed in Great Britain
by Biddles Ltd, Guildford, Surrey.

For Fiona,
another promise fulfilled

Acknowledgements

A book of this type is never simply the work of the author. Apart from the men who feature in it, special thanks must go to Frank Mayes for his whole-hearted and enthusiastic support and to his wife, Iris, for her kindness and hospitality. As a result of the atrocious weather that kept me firmly in Torbay for several weeks during a crucial development period, the research work in the North East was very capably undertaken by Stuart Davidson of Whitley Bay. Mike Esau has again been very much involved with the photographic research and my amanuensis, Ursula Waterman, has dealt with my longhand with the minimum of fuss and has never failed to deliver the typescript on time.

Finally, to my wife, Sally, a special word of thanks for her tolerance, understanding and encouragement.

Peter Grafton

Three Counties
Paignton
Devon

Contents

Illustrations

I
King's Cross

I stood at the end of platform 10 late one Saturday evening in October 1964 very much aware that I was witnessing, along with a crowd of several hundred people, the end of an era. The arrivals side of the station was intermittently illuminated by the brilliant white light from scores of flashbulbs, as though lightning was playing around the girders of Lewis Cubitt's graceful arches. Then with a blast on the chime whistle, the last A4 to visit King's Cross, 60009, 'Union of South Africa', reversed slowly out of the station and disappeared into Gasworks tunnel.

A romantic view? Perhaps so but then King's Cross and its environs have always had a touch of the romantic about them, at least for the dedicated LNER enthusiast. I gave my wife her engagement ring on platform 10 with A3 60061, 'Pretty Polly', as a backdrop – how much more romantic than that can one be?

Whatever sense of time or of history that I have was polarised when I presented myself at the King's Cross traction inspectors' office. Very little can have changed since Gresley's time. The office furniture is solid Edwardian: the heating is so inadequate that the first person in the office in the mornings lights the gas ring and puts a brick on top of it, but it is the walls that are eye-catching. They are covered with photographs that trace the locomotive history of the LNER: a sepia tinted photograph of 1470 complete with dimensions and with Gresley's signature in one corner, the cab of 4472 with William Whitelaw, top hatted and wing collared leaning out of the window. Driver Sparshatt is alongside him and Gresley, looking very pleased with life is in the background. But I wasn't there to wallow in the past, I was there to talk to traction inspector George Whitham whose view of King's Cross and Top Shed is somewhat less idealised than mine.

George joined the LNER after war service with the Royal Navy. Although he came from a railway family he was never encouraged to follow in the footsteps of his grandfather and father – the former a driver based at Mexborough, the latter driving from King's Cross when George joined the company.

At the time, not only were the engines in poor condition but so was the track and three derailments a day at Top Shed were quite common. Promotion was rapid and after only four weeks' cleaning it was Fireman Whitham and in at the deep end. He was booked for a week with his father and on his first firing trip, down to Hertford with an N2, badly injured a finger by trapping it in the handbrake collar. 'You don't,' commented George, 'do that trick twice.' His first mainline trip was with a V2 down to Grantham firing to Bill Hoole. I asked George about this now legendary figure and he corroborated all that I'd heard from Frank Mayes.

1. The late Bill Hoole, doyen of East Coast Main Line enthusiasts, in the cab of A4 Pacific 60017, 'Silver Fox', at Hitchin on 7 May 1955. Although he delighted his fans with his cavalier approach to driving, his escapades did not always endear him to his colleagues. On this occasion Bill was working the 5 p.m. from King's Cross to Peterborough and Cambridge which split at Hitchin, and he had run the 31.9 miles from King's Cross in 35 mins 57 secs.

George paused for a few seconds before answering my question.

'He was magic,' he replies. 'Above all he was a gentleman. He'd take any fireman with him and if the fireman proved to be incompetent he'd do the firing himself.'

We then digressed somewhat and I asked George to define a good driver. 'It is, of course, a matter of opinion,' he answered, 'but from my point of view, a good driver ran the train as economically as possible and made the fireman's task easy.'

The allocation of sets of men to jobs was done in sequence from the least to the most important, relatively of course. These were referred to as 'links' or 'gangs' and, at the time that George was a fireman, were organised as follows:

No. 1 Link. Leeds and Newcastle lodge supplemented by turns to Peterborough, Grantham, Doncaster and York.

No. 2 Link. Peterborough, Grantham and Doncaster (stop link for men who opted not to lodge).

No. 3 Link. Peterborough and Grantham.

No. 4 Link (odd main line). Cambridge and Peterborough supplemented by empty coaching stock and shed duty turns.

2. A4 Pacific 60009, 'Union of South Africa', photographed at Peterborough on 24 October 1964. The headboard gives details of the event: it is worth noting that on the return trip to King's Cross from Newcastle, 108 mph was recorded on Stoke bank, that the author was struggling with a bowl of soup at the time and that King's Cross was reached some 28 minutes early! Those of us present had the satisfaction of seeing the up 'Talisman', Deltic-hauled, turned inside south of Peterborough to allow the steam-hauled special to overtake.

No. 5 Link. Suburban passenger work. No night work and all crews had their regular engines which were cleaned voluntarily by some of the crews.

No. 6 Link (push and pull). Highgate and Alexandra Palace.

No. 7 Link. High Barnet, Edgware and South London, plus some suburban work. On Sundays there were some workings to Victoria via the city widened Lines.

1A Link (goods lodge). Came into being follow-ing the introduction of lodging in 1948, as did No. 1 Link in form shown above. 1A Link was interposed between No. 1 and No. 2 Links.

'Invariably V2 jobs,' said George. 'We'd rarely fewer than 60 wagons on and two particular turns come to mind: the 2 a.m. off King's Cross Goods Yard to York with a stop at Doncaster for examination and the 3.35 p.m. off King's Cross Goods Yard, also for York also with a booked stop at Doncaster. The 2 a.m. was fairly straightforward,' he went on, 'and we

3

3. A3 Pacific 60061, 'Pretty Polly', waiting to leave King's Cross with the 'White Rose' on 18 May 1963. Note the Deltic lurking in the background.

always worked the fish back from York. It was always reckoned to be a "Royal" fish and it ran to time, sometimes with only one wagon on. On the other hand, the 3.35 p.m. could be a nightmare. We'd get tangled up with rush hour traffic and we were frequently turned inside. It was not uncommon to wait for three hours at Ricall and we were hand to mouth for water to York.

'We had an odd Hull job in that link,' he continued, 'usually a B1. They didn't ride well and the management had a tendency to use mixed traffic engines for harder jobs than were intended. I found them impossible to "nurse" because if you pulled them back below 25 per cent cut off, they'd go off the boil.'

The top link at King's Cross covered the Newcastle jobs and the prestige trains. There were 18 sets of men in the link working an 18 week cycle. Progression through the links took little account of competence, although some top link drivers would ask for certain firemen if it was known that promotion was in the offing. It was a natural progression based on

4

4. An evening view of King's Cross on 3 June 1957. An L1 leaves with a local train consisting of two sets of 'quad articulated', and a single coach. An A4 stands in the foreground, partially obscured by a goods van. Scott's Gothic tower of St Pancras presides over the scene.

seniority and the fact that it appeared to be structured from the 'Met' link through to Newcastle working was coincidental. As George observed, 'By the time you'd moved through the links from the "Met" to Newcastle, a Grantham trip seemed like a shunt!'

Having reached the top link, George had a regular mate – George Tee – and a regular engine A4 60017, 'Silver Fox'. This was a single blast pipe A4 and according to George, 'It was a good engine and it would burn bricks.' Later on the two Georges were given A4 60034, 'Lord Faringdon'.

Talk then turned, inevitably I suppose, to George's experiences in the top link. He used a turn on the 'Flying Scotsman' as an example of a typical working day and as with all experts, whatever their discipline, he made it sound very easy.

'We booked on at 8.30 a.m.,' he said, 'and we

5. Holloway bank. An N7/5, working hard, overtakes an N2/2 that is, according to the destination board, heading for Hatfield.

were allowed an hour for engine preparation. By 9.30 a.m. I'd made up the fire, topped up the tender with coal and ideally had about an inch and a half of water showing in the gauge class. As we moved off from the shed, I'd make sure that she wasn't blowing off and not making any smoke. We'd be away from the Cross on time with no more than half a glass of water and the exhaust injector on. As soon as we'd cleared the tunnels I'd start firing and fire steadily to Potters Bar. Then I'd have a rest as far as Woolmer Green and prepare for a dip at Langley – this was a routine. It was important at all the troughs that you didn't run the tanks over, otherwise you'd be 800 or 1,000 gallons light and it was a long haul from Scrooby troughs to your next dip at

6

6. Down fitted freight hauled by V2 60954 north of Little Bytham on 14 April 1953.

Hugh Ballant

7. A4 Pacific 60029, 'Woodcock', on the up 'Norseman' near Stoke tunnel in 1961.

Wiske Moor. With my own engine I could judge it quite well – it wasn't so easy with a strange engine. You see with my own engine I used to keep the mechanism of the scoop well lubricated and I knew how many turns of the handle it took to skim the water. I remember one chap who got a piece of cotton waste caught in the scoop handle, couldn't raise it and picked up all the AWS magnets down to Hitchin.

'As far as coal was concerned, if you had a good mate you wouldn't have to fetch any forward before York. After York you'd be stretching for it and it was 41 miles of non-stop firing to Darlington.

'We had an engine change at Newcastle and I'd start running her down at Durham and hope that we wouldn't be checked by signals. Ideally, you'd have a full boiler, 250 lbs of steam and be

8

8. V2s at Top Shed; King's Cross on 27 February 1960. 60800, 'Green Arrow', is now preserved as LNER 4771 at Steamtown, Carnforth.

able to push the fire forward. Then I'd get out the bucket and have a wash. Of course, if we got a signal check, I'd have to pick up the shovel and start again. We had a similar procedure coming back – I used to reckon that if I'd a full boiler, 250 lbs on the clock and Welwyn's distant off, I'd finished. I'd put the pricker in, get the fire from the back corners and under the door and then get the bucket out. Provided we weren't checked we'd run into King's Cross with about 200 lbs showing, an inch of water in the glass and she'd stand in the station for three hours if necessary.

'When we got to Newcastle we were relieved straight away – this was an agreement concerning lodging turns. We'd work back next day with the 9.25 a.m. or the up "Scotsman". Provided there was nothing wrong with the engine we'd gone down with we'd bring her back. Invariably Gateshead would use her during the night – perhaps a parcels to York and back.

'We were booked off on arrival at King's Cross but due to shortage of men it didn't always work out that way. On top of that there was always congestion at Top Shed, especially after the evening peak periods. It was nothing to

9

9. The sole representative of its class, W1 4–6–4 60700. This locomotive, which was never named, did some sterling work on the East Coast Main Line. It was rebuilt from Gresley's experimental, high pressure water tube boiler locomotive and is shown here passing Hornsey with a down Leeds express on 24 May 1958.

be at the end of a queue of eight or nine locos at Holloway and wait for hours on end. I once waited 11 hours after an eight hour shift on the "Met" and I've been 2–2½ hours in the station waiting for relief.'

Our conversation then turned to the working of 'The Elizabethan'. 'I never really liked the non-stops,' said George, although he and Frank Mayes were in complete agreement about the down working. 'It was,' said George, 'a snip but the up working was hard graft.'

At King's Cross, the engine off the up

10

10. A4 Pacific 60028, 'Walter K. Whigham' (originally 'Sea Eagle'), approaching Peterborough with the up 'Flying Scotsman' on 16 April 1953. Note the GNR warning notice on the water crane.

Les Perrin

'Elizabethan' was serviced in the passenger locomotive depot and the tender was filled with a special type of coal. After that it went to Top Shed for examination and next morning after the fire had been made up, the engine was taken under the coal hopper and the tender was topped up. So, with a fresh engine and a clean fire, the crew was off to a flying start.

King's Cross and Haymarket adopted different practices with regard to the servicing and maintenance of locomotives allocated to the non-stop trains. At Edinburgh, the engine came off the train and went straight under the coal hopper and was coaled with whatever came out. As a result, working the up non-stop could have its problems. On one occasion with A4 60034, 'Lord Faringdon', George's predecessor had emptied his tender and swept it out by the time he got to Barnet. The train reached King's Cross but the fire went out whilst the engine was standing in the station. George maintained that the King's Cross men had a cleaner fire on arrival than did the Haymarket men on arrival in Edinburgh.

There was a variation in the practice of allocating engines to the non-stop: King's Cross

11

11. Another view of Peterborough with A1 Pacific 60149, 'Amadis', passing North box with an up express for King's Cross in 1957. The A1s were the final form of 6′ 8″ coupled wheel Pacifics to work over the East Coast Main Line and the LNER ancestry can be clearly seen in this photograph.

would take two engines that were ex-works, run them in and then use them for non-stop workings whereas Haymarket would allocate engines that were well run-in and give them a thorough examination.

The non-stop workings were regarded as prestigious by some of the men who would go to the extent of altering their holidays to ensure that they didn't miss a turn. The crews would be rostered to it for a week at a time and had a special rate of pay. They were guaranteed eight hours per day, plus four hours mileage and an extra eight hours per week giving a total of 123¾ hours. In addition they had meals on the train and, of course, a reserved compartment.

On the down journey, the Haymarket men

12

12. A4 60034, 'Lord Faringdon' (originally 'Peregrine'), ex-works and pristine at Doncaster in June 1955. The photograph shows the smoke-box door inside the 'cod's mouth' opening and it also shows clearly the inspection panels on the boiler casing.

would come through the tender and relieve the King's Cross crew at York – somewhat short of the actual half-way mark but more convenient than the booked point, as the train was travelling at a restricted speed through the station. The King's Cross men would then go back to their compartment, wash and change and go to the dining car for lunch. Round about Berwick, the King's Cross fireman would take a can of tea to the engine for the Scottish crew.

On the up journey it was always something of a rush for the London men. The dining car staff had only just begun to serve lunch by Durham and, 'It was,' said George, 'a scramble from Darlington to get changed, get up the front and then indigestion all the way.' Sunday workings on the non-stop were something of a misnomer. Apart from a booked stop at York, permanent way checks were frequent and these played havoc with the fire. 'You finished with a box full and not much steam,' said George. 'Talking of Sunday workings,' he went on, 'I remember going down to Newcastle on the 10 o'clock with number 13 [A4 60013, "Dominion of New Zealand"] and the troughs at Langley were out of use. We had a dip at Werrington at the same time as 149 [A1 60149, "Amadis"] on the up road. He'd come up from Grantham and was

13

13. Contrasting front ends at King's Cross on 10 June 1960. This photograph shows both the differences and the similarities between A3 Pacific 60106, 'Flying Fox', and A1 Pacific 60155, 'Borderer'.   *Ian S Carr*

anxious to get a full tank. He dipped as soon as he got on the troughs and ran the tank over straight away. He took our front window out, the side spectacle and bent the corridor door a foot the wrong side of the lock. We had to come off at Grantham and if I hadn't been at the other side working the scoop I wouldn't be talking to you now. It was just water that did it – he didn't bring any coal down. We had to come off because of the broken window and we couldn't get into the corridor to get the fire irons. Actually he did us a good turn because she was off the boil. We'd have had a struggle because she wasn't free steaming and with only 210 lbs at Peterborough, if that's the best she could do, we'd have been in trouble by Durham.'

I asked George if he ever worried about the risks inherent in working on a steam loco-motive. 'It might be something you thought of to start with but you soon forgot it. I was going

14

down on 28 [A4 60028, "Walter K. Whigham"] one day when the pipe to the pressure gauge went. I just hammered the pipe with a spanner and we carried on to Newcastle. Of course we'd try to prevent things happening – I changed the gauge glasses on my regular engine every eight weeks but then things happened that couldn't be prevented. 10000 (BR 60700, W1 4–6–4) had just come out of Stoke tunnel one day when the main steam pipe fractured. It blew ash through the firebox door which almost blinded the driver – he ended his days on the railway on shunting duties. His fireman was lucky, he got out onto the framing.'

Not so lucky, however, was the fireman involved in a blow back in Wood Green tunnel. He was working a V2 with a heavy train and said George, 'He had his head down and was firing when it happened. He was burnt internally as well as externally and was found wandering in Southgate Yard. He had treatment in East Grinstead Hospital, was off work for a year or more and ended his railway days in the stores – he never went back on the footplate.'

The accident was caused by the fittings of the spark arrester falling across the blastpipe when the engine was being worked hard in the tunnel. The irony here was that the spark arrester had been removed as it interfered with the steaming of the engine.

The interview over, I had a cup of tea in the inspectors' office and with a final look at the photographs, I went to the door.

'Did you get up from Devon all right this morning?' enquired one of George's colleagues. I explained that I had travelled up the previous day and had spent the night at Romford with Frank Mayes and his family. 'Well, I hope you get back all right,' he said, 'because there's a guards' strike at Paddington. You'd best give Frank a ring at Liverpool Street and ask for another night's lodging.' I prized my son away from the end of the platform and we made our way to Paddington. Fortunately, we caught one of the very few West of England trains that ran that day and we passed the journey to Paignton listening to the tapes and talking LNER – what better way to travel over the Great Western?

2
South Yorkshire

Tom Hobson had a fine baritone voice and was much in demand at charity concerts. Bill Pace was tall, cultured and had aspirations towards serving on the local council. Arthur Wray was very much a political animal and, as a socialist in the correct sense, he it was who influenced my political thinking and I've been to the right of centre ever since that first post-war election. These three names are taken at random from a group of railwaymen who were working in and around Barnsley during the 1939–45 war and with whom, at various times, I spent hours on the footplates of locomotives as diverse in types as the men who crewed them.

I recall standing at the end of Barnsley Court House station one summer evening in 1944 when a C13 approached from the direction of Barnsley Junction. It slowed down to a walking pace and Tom Hobson leaned out and shouted to me, 'Do you fancy a trip to Stairfoot and back?' There was only one answer and as we rattled away past Barnsley West he treated his fireman, myself and anyone within earshot to 'The Road to Mandalay'. I cannot remember why the C13 – and according to my notes it was 5193 – was sent to Stairfoot and back, but I do remember being in a spot of trouble when I arrived home late. Fortunately, Tom Hobson lived only four doors away and he was able to speak for me.

Coincidentally, Bill Pace lived four doors further up the road and whilst Tom Hobson was working out of Jumble Lane, Bill Pace was allocated to Wentworth and was, amongst other duties, firing the 'Garratt'. He was a great mutual improvement class man and used to hold forth on the footplate on the techniques of firing, steam raising and the calorific values of various types of coal. Arthur Wray was in the same link as Bill Pace. A bachelor at the time, he was very friendly with my parents and so I saw quite a lot of him on and off the footplate. As I said, he was very politically minded and used to get himself involved in arguments with my mother. She came from a staunch Baptist–Liberal background and as far as I remember, he rarely won!

Other names come to mind. Arthur Crossley who walked from his home in Barnsley to his booking-on point at Stairfoot and back again, irrespective of the weather. 'Qual' Hall of dark and gloomy aspect. Frank Stainrod, Garratt driver and poacher extraordinary. He was a schoolboy's dream – he didn't care who drove the engine if there was the outside chance of bagging a rabbit or two. 'Knock 'em over on the way up, pick 'em up on the way back.' He died, tragically, on the Worsbrough branch line at Wentworth, the victim of one of his engines.

From this galaxy of LNER enginemen, some of them dead, most of them now retired, one stands out – one of them who lifted his sights beyond Jumble Lane and Wentworth Junction, Frank Mayes. He has been successful and happy

14. C13 4–4–2T 7404 arrives at Barnsley Court House station with a two-coach local from Penistone on 18 April 1947.

in his career, a career that started in 1943 by sheer chance. As a boy he worked in a local colliery and on being made redundant was sent by the Ministry of Labour and National Service to Jumble Lane depot as a cleaner. The locomotive stud at that time consisted of N5 and C13 tank engines 0–8–0 and 0–6–0 tender engines and a few 'Austerity' 2–8–0s stored for the War Department.

Working conditions at Jumble Lane were never ideal and night shift during the war made them even worse. The cleaning gang made the best of a bad job and Frank recalls an incident that not only underlines the point but emphasises the discipline that was enforced by management. One of his fellow cleaners threatened Frank with the contents of a fire-bucket and eventually cornered him in the messroom. Unfortunately, the shot went wide of the mark and the water knocked several tea bottles off the messroom stove. The foreman arrived and promptly booked the lads off duty. There was no arguing, no reasoning just a curt order to book off and to go home. That meant no pay for that night and Frank recalls that one of the cleaners was too frightened to go home and face his mother, so he spent the night until 6.00 a.m. wandering around the town.

A favourite trick, particularly if there was a new entrant to the cleaning gang, was to wait

17

15. J11 0–6–0 64425 photographed outside Barnsley shed on 24 June 1956.   *E H Sawford*

until he had gone into a firebox to clean the ends of tubes, clean the brick arch and remove damaged firebars, and then quickly close the firebox door. Somebody would put a slate over the chimney and a piece of smouldering waste in the ashpan, and those privy to what was going on would derive some pleasure from the discomfiture of the cleaner trapped in the firebox. Frank said that he fell victim to this procedure but in his case it didn't go quite as planned.

'I thought I'd get 'em a bit worried,' he told me, 'so I didn't shout or make a noise. I squatted in one corner of the box and waited. "Frank, are you all right in there?" No answer. A hurried conference on the footplate and the firebox door was flung open. As the head came in,' went on Frank, 'I grabbed it by the hair and hung on until they promised not to do it again.'

Promotion was rapid at this particular stage of the war and after only four months of cleaning, Frank was passed for firing. He recalls that the procedure was somewhat imprecise but that there was invariably an air of excitement about the mess room – who was going where and with whom. The drivers booked on with their regular firemen who were passed to drive and if more drivers were required than were available, then the passed firemen would be allocated to driving duties. In this event, the senior passed cleaner would go as fireman to the senior driver. So there was a situation where the men were reporting for duty not knowing where they were going, and what time they would book off. The running foreman would enquire about booked time and route knowledge and then issue the orders. It might be Godley or Mottram with a 2–8–0 or, with any luck, it might be Dunford and the possibility of two to three

18

16. Another view of Barnsley shed. 04/2 2–8–0 63883 stands on the shed road on 13 April 1957 whilst an unidentified tank locomotive waits in the platform of Barnsley (Exchange) station with a train for Wakefield. At the time that this photograph was taken Barnsley boasted four stations – Court House, Exchange, Summer Lane and Stairfoot. On the closure of Court House, Summer Lane and Stairfoot, Exchange became simply 'Barnsley'.

17. The largest locomotive to work on any British railway, the Gresley-Beyer-Peacock 'Garratt', stands at Wentworth Junction awaiting its next spell of duty in April 1947. Note the four vertical bolts in the foreground – preparation for the electrification of the line.

18. Hard at work, the 'Garratt' banks 04/8 3672 and a freight train towards Silkstone in April 1947. Much of the steelwork seen spanning the track was completed in 1939 and then work on the electrification scheme was suspended at the outbreak of the war.

hours overtime waiting inside at Bullhouse Loop. On the other hand it might be junior passed cleaners to the ash pit or the coal stage.

Frank's second firing turn was, he asserts, more memorable than his first. He reported to Barnsley for orders on a foggy January morning and was told by Sid Wood, the foreman, that he was to fire to Jack Hawcroft and to go to Wath. 'Now Jack was a man of few words,' said Frank, 'but he did express surprise when I told him how old I was. He grumbled about it and the bus journey to Wath passed in silence. At Wath we relieved the crew of an "Austerity" 2–8–0 and set off for Mottram. I'd no idea how to fire the engine and as we trundled along the steam pressure dropped. So now the driver had two problems, a green fireman and fog. We picked up a banker at Wombwell and this did some-thing to help. We had a signal check at Strafford crossing and Jack examined the fire. "Tha's got a bloody 'aycock there," he grunted. He grabbed the clinker shovel, levelled the fire out over the bars and in no time at all the pressure was rising and the injector was on.'

After 250 firing turns it was customary for the fireman to be given the '250 test'. In Frank's case he worked the 1.20 p.m. Barnsley Court House to Penistone accompanied by an inspector. Following the practical part of the test was an oral test and having passed, the junior rate of pay for firemen was confirmed. The successful candidate was also given a serge jacket and a cap. The next hurdle was to complete 313 firing turns after which fireman's rate was paid even if allocated to shed duties.

Goods and freight workings were particularly heavy during the period 1944–6 as a result of extra traffic generated by the war. The crews

20

19. An 04/3 drifts down the bank towards Wentworth Junction in April 1947. This locomotive was one of Robinson's 'no-nonsense' designs for the War Office and was introduced in 1917.

were used as required and not diagrammed. Passenger turns were obviously more predictable and one regular job for passed cleaners was the 1.20 Barnsley–Penistone returning at 2.20. This was a train that ran specifically for the workers at David Brown's factory and coincided with the 6–2, 2–10 shift changeover.

In 1946, traffic decreased and Frank was back in the cleaning gang. A vacancy arose at Wentworth Junction and under the LNER 'pocket system' he applied for it and was transferred to Wentworth as a fireman. The pocket system was a method of safeguarding promotion within an area or pocket. A local vacancy would be advertised within the pocket and when it was filled the vacancy thus created would be advertised generally. In Frank's case, a vacancy occurred at Barnsley and one of the Wentworth men applied for it and was successful. Frank then applied to fill the vacancy left at Wentworth. From his point of view, it was a good move as he was established as a fireman and his home was within sight of the booking-on point at Wentworth Junction.

Conditions at Wentworth were considered to be easy. The reconstruction of Woodhead Tunnel caused the diversion of much of the traffic via the former L and Y line through

H C Casserley

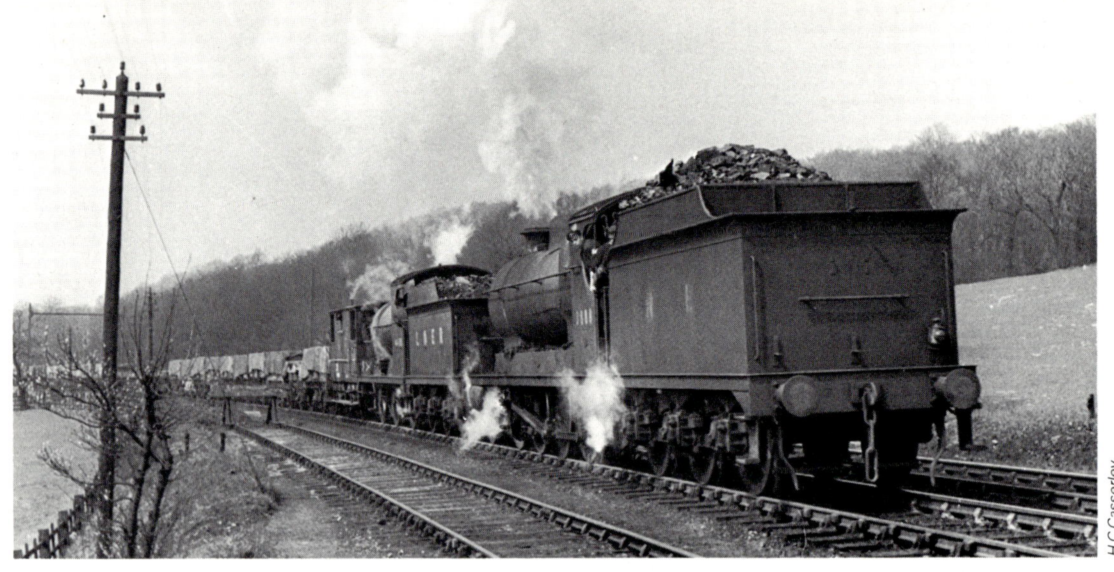

20. An unusual combination on banking duties on the Worsbrough branch line. 04/8 2–8–0 6388 gives assistance to un-rebuilt J11 0–6–0 64400 in April 1947.

21. S1/1 0–8–4T 69902 shunting in Wath yard. Note the express passenger lamps on the front buffer beam. This photograph was taken in August 1953 just before diesel shunters replaced steam.

H C Casserley

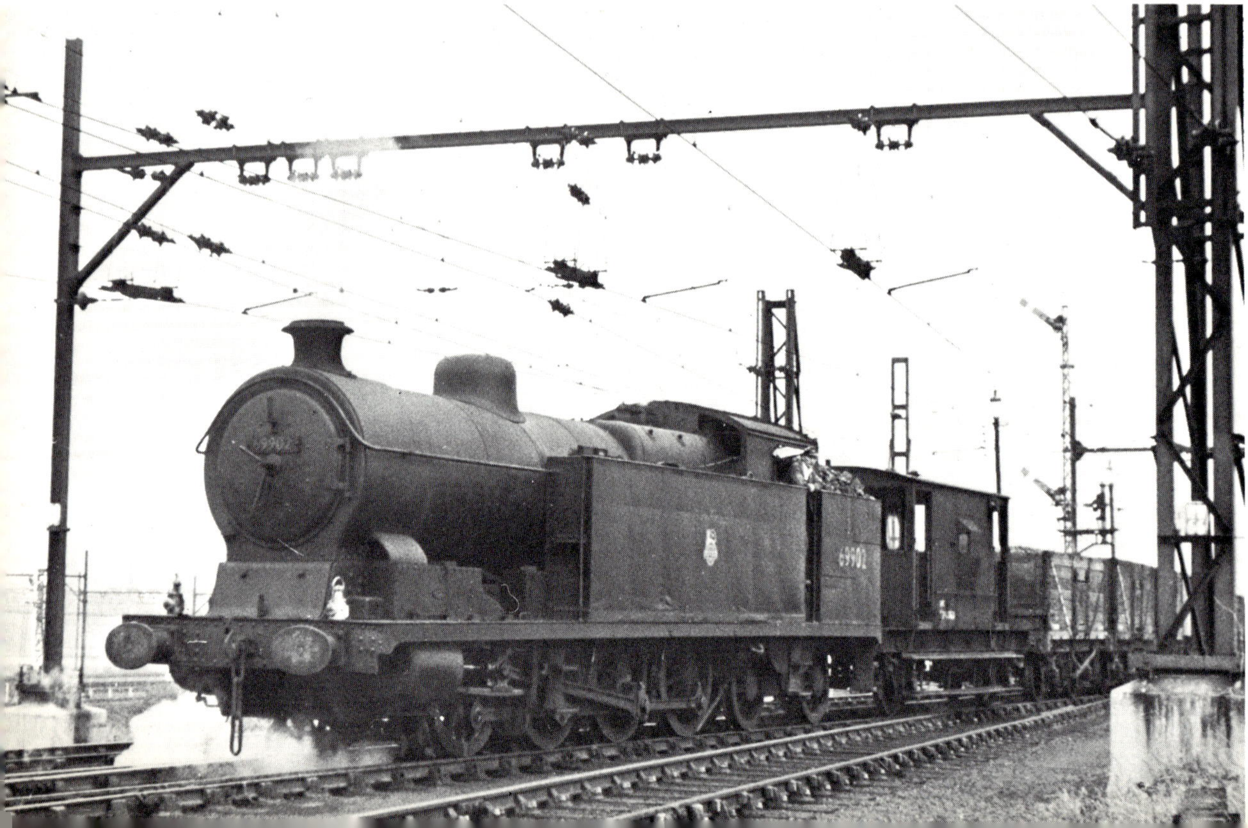

Barnsley and Wakefield and as a result, the nine sets of men at Wentworth were not over-worked. The motive power consisted of 04s, War Department 2–8–0s, LMS 8Fs, some of which were built at Doncaster, and Gresley's biggest one-off job, the Garratt. The loco-motives were used on banking duties as required and so, with three sets of men per shift and no supervision, it will be appreciated that it was a pleasant enough existence for the crews and an absolute haven for a 12-year-old schoolboy, whose infatuation with the steam locomotive was turning into love!

Although I rode up and down the line be-tween Wentworth Junction and West Silkstone Junction more times than I can remember, I was only vaguely aware of problems created by the Garratt. It was the biggest steam locomotive ever built for a British railway and was, I suppose, a fairly typical example of Gresley's muddled thinking in some areas of locomotive design. That he didn't think through the P1s is an accepted fact; he thought even less about the implications in introducing the Garratt. Fortu-nately, Frank Mayes is more objective about it than I am and he explained in detail to me the arrangements for working it and the agreements that had been negotiated with management by the unions.

The men were rostered to the Garratt on a nine week cycle. For the first three weeks they would work Mondays and Thursdays, week one 10 – 6, week two 2 – 10 and week three 6 – 2. The next three weeks they would work Wednesdays and Saturdays and then, to round off the cycle, three weeks of Tuesdays and Fridays. As the loco was out of service on Sundays there was no Sunday working and the men did not work two consecutive days or more than two days per week on the engine. There was no extra pay for Garratt working although it had, arguably, the largest hand fired firebox in

Europe. Frank says that he lost more sweat on the Garratt than he ever did firing A4s.

The stretch of line over which the Garratt worked was about 2½ miles long with a ruling gradient of 1 in 40. Banking of heavy mineral trains was usually done with two 2–8–0s and the Garratt working very hard up the bank as far as Silkstone West Junction. Occasionally they would go through to Oxspring Junction if the train was exceptionally heavy or if the train engine was in trouble. Also, on occasions, the Garratt would be used to assist trains descending the bank. The normal procedure was to stop the train at Silkstone West, pin down the brakes on the first eight wagons and thereafter on every third wagon. But sparks from the brake blocks were considered to be a hazard when tanker wagons and timber built wagons loaded with bombs were in the train. Under these circum-stances the Garratt would be attached to the train engine and assist with braking as far as Wentworth Junction.

Normal servicing of the Garratt was done at Wentworth and the engine went to Mex-borough every Sunday for a routine inspection and boiler washout, returning to Wentworth in time for the 6 – 2 shift on Mondays. On occasions it went to Barnsley Jumble Lane for its weekend rest – these visits were usually due to engineering or p.w. work between Wentworth and Mexborough. I have a vivid recollection of the Garratt dominating Jumble Lane crossing one Sunday morning during the war. It was a big enough engine in all conscience at Went-worth, but seen out of its usual environment and in totally different surroundings it was awe-inspiring.

Coaling arrangements for the stud of loco-motives at Wentworth were made with the management of a very conveniently sited drift mine. A single line spur came off the main line to the east of Wentworth Junction box and led to a

H C Casserley

22. Yet another 04/3: this time 63744 waits at Mexborough with a train of coal empties.

coaling stage at the mine. The engines would take coal as necessary, the fireman collecting the staff from the signalman before proceeding down the severely curved line at little more than walking pace.

Frank relates the story of the inexperienced fireman who was told by his driver to clean the fire of the Garratt before going for coal. The fireman carried out his duties so assiduously that the fire went out and the driver discovered him in a state of near panic trying to re-light it. As can be imagined the driver left his mate in no doubt about his incompetence, at which point a platelayer approached the engine and asked the driver what he thought about his new fireman. Now the platelayer was the fireman's father, a fact unknown to the driver. The platelayer listened patiently to the driver's comments and then swinging his hammer onto his shoulder left with the words, 'Aye, well, he's like his mother – a bit slow.'

In 1949 unions and management agreed on conditions for redundancy and transfer and by February 1950 the pocket system was phased out. This affected Wentworth in so far as all senior firemen had to be passed for driving, so that it could become a depot in its own right and not an 'outpost' of Barnsley. Frank attended mutual improvement classes on Wednesdays and Sundays throughout 1950 and passed for driving at the end of the year, just in time to see the first section of the Wath – Manchester electrification scheme come into operation. The inevitable happened, the Wentworth men were made redundant in October 1951 and Frank applied for a transfer to King's Cross. As redundant men took priority when applying for vacancies, the transfer was almost foregone and Frank started in the junior express goods link at King's Cross on 4 February 1952. He says that he was pleased to go for many reasons – not least of which was that he had married a London girl,

24

whom he had met whilst on holiday in Wales in 1948, and was thus able to continue with his work on the railway.

Frank recalls his early days at Top Shed as being a period of re-adjustment. He had no experience of main line working and his first driver was less than helpful. He struggled back from Cambridge with an ailing B1 and then received another experience – cockney humour. 'I was,' Frank said, 'still firing on the assumption that I only had three miles up the bank.' Fortunately, his fellow firemen were helpful and he then spent 12 weeks in the Doncaster link with Bill Hoole with whom he got on very well.

'Bill was a great help and like me he was railway mad,' Frank said. 'He was a hard driver, sure he was, but he was a hard worker and a good mate. He'd take his turn with the shovel and give me every encouragement to drive. I learned a lot from Bill and a lot from messroom conversations.'

Progress through the links was steady until Frank arrived in the top express passenger link and fired to Sid Tappin. 'I worked with Sid for three years and we never had a wrong word. During that time we had our own engine A4, "Woodcock", 60020 and worked "The Eliza-bethan". One thing I always remember about Sid was his philosophy if you were in trouble with your engine. "Never whistle for another engine because if you do, the chances are you'll get another bad 'un." Only once did he break this rule and proved the point. We were on the up Tyne-Tees Pullman and had problems all the way to Peterborough where we came off and they gave us a Thompson A2/1 – enough said.'

Frank's firing career ended in 1956 when he became a spare driver. He signed the road to Peterborough, Grantham and Doncaster and on one memorable occasion did a trip to York with A3 60055.

'We'd had a lot of rain,' he said, 'and the driver rostered to this particular job didn't turn up. In addition, the tunnels at King's Cross were flooded and things were chaotic. I had a very poor trip because the loco was in poor shape – injector trouble.'

In 1958 Frank transferred to the GE section and was based at Stratford. Since then he has become a traction inspector and as he put it, 'I've come full circle. When I was in the messroom at Barnsley I didn't know where I was going from day to day and when I go to my office at Liverpool Street, the same thing applies.'

3
Heaton and York

This section starts a long way from York – in the messroom of the Torbay and Kingswear Railway, Queens Park Station, Paignton in 1973. 'Flying Scotsman' was a summer visitor that year and with her was a back-up team of technical and commercial experts. I was a volunteer worker doing anything that was required of me in the locomotive department. On the afternoon that I have in mind I went to the messroom for a wash, a cup of tea and, as I considered, a well-earned cigarette. Now the messroom never was luxurious – I suppose the management reasoned that if it was too comfortable, the volunteers would be loath to leave it. As it was, it required a strong constitution to go in. Anyway, on this particular occasion I was somewhat taken aback at the sight of a spare, almost ascetic man carrying out a series of yoga-like exercises on one of the benches. His right leg was horizontal on the bench, his left leg at a right angle to it and his head was resting on his right knee. He sat up as I crossed the threshold grinned at me and with a marked Geordie accent asked me if I could do that. I had to admit that I thought he had the advantage over me and that was how I met Les Richards. From that rather unusual meeting developed a friendship that has continued over the years and will, I hope, continue for many years to come.

Like several of the men whom I have interviewed whilst working on this series of books, Les Richards became a railwayman by default. The return of men from the First World War made Les redundant and, living as he did in a remote part of north-west Durham, it was either the railway or nothing and so on 12 August 1919 he became an engine cleaner on the NER.

It is unlikely that the name Waskerley will mean much to many people. It is a small community south-west of Consett and yet it was, in the 1920s, quite an important railway centre. When Les Richards joined the depot staff it had an allocation of 13 locomotives and he remembers the first one on which he worked – it was a McDonnell 0–6–0 number 498. At the time there were six cleaners employed, four on day shift and two on nights. The day shift men were expected to assist the fitters and the night shift men were expected to assist the steam raiser. After 12 months of cleaning duties, Les experienced his first firing turn and became a passed cleaner in 1921.

So far as the railway was concerned, the area was developed to work limestone from the Stanhope quarries to the Consett Iron Co.'s works. In addition there was a line from Rookhope lead mines to Blanchland (originally Parkhead) along which lead ore was transported, the emphasis being on mineral traffic. There was, however, one passenger train working which was a double shift job from Darlington to Blackhill. The early turn crew prepared

23. A3 Pacific 4472, 'Flying Scotsman', passing Paignton goods station – now demolished – with the 10.15 a.m. for Kingswear, 21 July 1973.

P J Lynch

24. Raven-designed B16/1 61451 at York with a very mixed freight train on 21 April 1961. As built, these locomotives had Stephenson link motion actuating the valves and were a fitter's nightmare – there were six eccentrics and a big end between the frames.

three class B tank engines and their own engine, usually a class F and then worked light engine to Blackhill. They worked the train to Darlington and back to Burnhill where they were relieved by the late shift crew, who then worked Blackhill – Darlington – Blackhill and back to the depot for disposal.

The locomotive stud consisted of class F, class B, 1090 class and 398 class. Engines 856 and 136 were often based at Consett Junction along with some of the 398s and were on pilot and shunting duties in Consett Yard and in Consett Junction Yard. This was relieved by a Sundays only passenger turn from Blackhill to Newcastle. The morning trip was via the Derwent Valley – Rowlands Gill – Swalwell to Newcastle

Brian Morrison

25. Heaton MPD in August 1954. V2 2–6–2 60810 passes with a van train for York as Ivatt 4MT 43016 emerges from the shed.

and the afternoon trip came back via Annfield, a route known to the engineers as 'The Alps' because two parts of it were 1 in 35.

Les was made redundant as a fireman in 1929 shortly after he was married. He had been earning £3 6s 0d (£3.30) per week as a fireman, but he was put back to cleaner's grade and his wage reduced to £2 17s 0d (£2.85) per week. He recalls that he was allocated to coal picking – loading coal from stock piles into wagons – and worked a three day week. The union had guaranteed a four day week so there was an extra 2s 6d (12½p) on top of the pay for three days. If, however, the men worked four days the unions did not make a contribution. Now Sunday was not included in the agreement, so if the men worked Sunday plus three days they received four days pay plus the 2s 6d from the union.

29

H N James

26. Q6 63427 at Consett Ironworks on 6 August 1962.

27. Consett station in the autumn of 1963. Note the locomotive at the head of the train of iron-ore empties.

H C Casserley

28. Two 9Fs working hard with a Tyne Dock–Consett Ironworks train of iron ore.

Les could not see much of a future in north-west Durham, 'And I didn't fancy shovelling coal for donkey's years,' he said, so he applied for a transfer to Normanton as a fireman. This job lasted for about nine months and Les remembers that the work was rather monotonous. It consisted of pilot duties at Castleford, in and out of Monk Fryston colliery with coal traffic and on Sundays only a turn to Hull with a passenger working and a class R locomotive. Anxious to get back to the North-East, Les transferred to Consett and in 1935 when conditions again became very bad he went to Blaydon. This job lasted about six months and then came another move to Heaton.

At the time Heaton was an important depot with a variety of locomotives including Pacifics. The usual links structure obtained and the bottom or lowest link was known as the 'dust' link. Under normal conditions, the crews in this link didn't prepare or stable engines because fire droppers were employed, but if one of them failed to report for duty then a dust link crew would be pressed into service and six engines had to be stabled, which was considered to be hard for the shift. If, however, demands for motive power were heavy, then the running foreman would allocate extra work. This could and did cause problems, as there was a tendency for the work to be rushed and there would be repercussions if an engine didn't steam well because the fire hadn't been cleaned properly.

31

After the dust link came the preparation link. As its name implies the crews in this link were given engines to prepare with details of the times that each was required.

'The worst job,' said Les, 'was the 12.01 on Monday morning, which was supposed to be a day shift turn. Believe me the shed was a mass of smoke and you could hardly see from one end of the engine to the other. You were keen enough to get on with your work and to get out for a bit of fresh air. You'd possibly be given two or three engines to start with and you got on with the job. When you'd finished that you went back and you had your bait and then went to see the running foreman. Perhaps he had another couple of engines for you and you progressed until you'd done your six engines.'

Although Gateshead depot covered most of the London – Edinburgh workings, Heaton had its share of main line passenger turns, including trips to Leeds, Doncaster and Edinburgh and an additional advantage at Heaton was the experience that was to be gained with electric traction.

The North Eastern Railway, urged on by that indefatigable champion of electric traction, Sir Vincent Raven, was the first major railway company in the country to tackle the problems of electrification. One of the earliest projects was the installation of overhead equipment into Trafalgar Yard and the electrification of the Newcastle – Tynemouth section. Perhaps the best remembered undertaking was the introduction of electric traction on the Shildon – Middlesbrough line, doomed in 1935 by a dramatic reduction in coal traffic and the heavy capital outlay required to replace ageing lineside equipment.

At the time that Les Richards was at Heaton, trains in and out of Trafalgar Yard and the Quayside branch at Newcastle were operated by electric locomotives and all the crews at the depot were taught the fundamentals of electric traction. When a fireman was rostered to the 'electric turns' he was responsible for loco-motive preparation. This involved ensuring that the pantograph was working properly, that the contactors were clean and that the sandboxes were filled. In addition, the traction motors had to be greased at the end of the shift.

The working was somewhat complicated be-cause on some sections the current was picked up via the pantograph, and some were energised via a third rail.

'It was,' said Les, 'a bit of a Heath Robinson affair coming away from the bottom of the bank into the tunnels but it wasn't so bad at the top. You could stand onto the rail, pull your bow (pantograph) down at leisure and put the pin in, pull out the bow stitch and then you were work-ing on your shoe (third rail contact). But when you were at the bottom, it was another kettle of fish altogether. When you got down, you put the bow up, put your switch in for the bow and pulled out the other one for the shoe. Now when you'd done all this, it was a heavy gradient and there was a mark on the wall before going into the tunnel and you put the switch in for the shoe and then waited for the mark and as soon as you got opposite it, you pulled the bow down and struggled to put the pin in to hold it. On occasions, the bow was knocked off. That meant you'd to put a steam pilot on – blue sparks and the lot.

'There was one driver, Jack Burke, who used to say 85 to 40 somebody knocks the bow off today and nine times out of ten it happened.'

Conversation then turned to drivers in general and some of the Heaton men in particular. The two who were outstanding so far as Les was concerned were Bill Lake and Jack Howie, the latter known to his colleagues as 'Captain Bligh' because of his footplate discipline.

'He had,' said Les, 'a way of his own and he

29. 9F 92060 with a Tyne Dock–Consett train at King Edward Bridge Junction, Gateshead on 1 May 1966.

Ian S Carr

was the driver and that was that. My job was to get steam and steam we got.'

The locomotive stock at Heaton was comprehensive – from J72s to Pacifics and footplate experience was varied as a result. This was particularly true of the 'spare' link. In Les's opinion the best job was the 18.20 Newcastle – Edinburgh and the 22.30 back. This meant that the crew was back in the depot and booked off by 00.30.

One day in April 1942 Les booked on for work at 04.00 and was told by the night shift supervisor that he had to report to the boss. This came as no surprise as he had, on the previous day, had a somewhat violent difference of opinion with the supervisor. So, expecting to be

33

30. 9F 92097 arrives at Consett and eases gently onto the iron-ore hoppers before discharging the wagons.

34

carpeted, Les was somewhat taken aback when he was asked if he would take on the duties of spare running foreman.

In 1945 he was promoted to East Coast Inspector working between Grantham – York – Newcastle and Edinburgh with responsibility for the investigation of bad time-keeping, particularly with respect to lost time.

'With regard to lost time,' said Les, 'we had to find out whose fault it was – train crews, locomotives, or serious signal delays or station delays which were a bane to a locomotive driver. You'd be two or three minutes late away from a station, yet on the station sheet you'd be down as left on time. This sort of thing invariably built up. Also you had variation in the time shown by clocks. You'd set away from, say, Newcastle at the right time but even when you got as far as Durham, 14 miles away, there'd be two minutes difference in the clocks. So we did our timings using our own watches.

'That was another thing I could never understand,' he mused. 'A guard was issued with a watch in order to time the train, but the man who did it had to find his own watch.'

During this period, 1945–50, conditions were slowly improving and when Les's next promotion came, he asserted that the locomotives, the Pacifics in particular, were 'in good nick'. In addition, he met the man whom he considers to be the best engineman that he ever knew – Bill Hogarth of Gateshead.

'He was,' said Les, 'a bit of a menace on the shed as he was a stickler for having things correct, but once you got him out onto the running road you couldn't beat him as an engineman. He was a real tip-top engineman – he was par excellence. In my opinion,' he continued, 'a good driver trains his fireman – there's co-ordination between them so that you have two men working practically as one. The fireman watches the way in which the driver runs his locomotive, not only with respect to the regulator handle which on a Pacific should always be wide open, but also where he was running his engine on the reversing quadrant. It's astonishing what two good men could get out of a locomotive compared with a poor or a moderate set of men. You've got to see it to appreciate it. Bill Hogarth was one of the best men I ever knew as a locomotive driver. He set out to get the best out of his engine, whether it was a good or a bad one, in the easiest possible way. Another tip-top man was George Robson – a man from whom I learned everything initially. Happily he's still alive and hale and hearty at 86.'

From being one of a team of four inspectors based at Newcastle, Les became headquarters inspector at Middlesbrough. Here, his area of responsibility included the introduction of diesel locomotives in the various yards in and around Teesside. Some of the drivers were less than happy about the advent of diesel shunters, and one of them went so far as to state that it was impossible for the job to be done with diesels.

'I took over the working myself on that particular morning,' said Les, 'and did the shunting for him. I then confronted the depot master with the fact that the job was completed and that we had time to spare, and I hoped that he was satisfied with the performance of the diesel. He couldn't say any other because the job had been completed in less time than he said was possible.'

Les attended a training course on diesels at Derby and became a member of the first team of inspectors to examine crews on diesel operation, and to test various types of locomotives at the factories before they were accepted by BR.

From Middlesbrough he went to York as examining inspector and it was back to steam. He was responsible for the examining of firemen before they were passed for driving. This in-

31. A8 4–6–2T 69859 leaves Darlington with the 5.56 p.m. for Saltburn via Middlesbrough on 28 August 1954. The A8s did sterling work in and around Darlington and were Gresley re-builds of Raven's D class 4–4–4T locomotives.

cluded rules and regulations, the mechanical aspects of the locomotive, especially the different types of brakes.

'You see it was a two day job,' he recalled. 'You examined a man on his rules and once he had satisfied you on these and on his oral examination, on the mechanical side, you did his run out next day.'

After five years as examining inspector Les was promoted to Chief Locomotive Inspector, North Eastern Region. In due course, the North Eastern and Eastern Regions were amalgamated and Les took over the Eastern Region from King's Cross to Berwick, with an office initially over the Coach and Horses in York. He was responsible for co-ordinating the work of a team of district inspectors and headquarters inspectors.

It was during this period that Les met Alan Pegler and as a result became a very important member of Flying Scotsman Enterprises, although this is anticipating somewhat.

During the mid and late 1960s 'Flying Scotsman' was out and about on BR hauling enthusiasts' specials. When she was operating over the Eastern Region Les had to allocate the

36

inspector or inspectors to ride with her and on occasions he allocated himself.

In the minds of many enthusiasts the culmination of 'Flying Scotsman's' feats was the fortieth anniversary of the first non-stop run to Edinburgh on 1 May 1968. At the time, I was involved with BR to the extent that I was having some difficulty in obtaining the co-operation that was necessary for me to research into the life and work of Edward Thompson. The wind of change that had blown through 222 Marylebone Road in the years between 1965 and 1968 was anti-steam to the point of being neurotic, and I was privately of the opinion that the fortieth anniversary run would be cancelled. In the event I was proved wrong, but I feel that it was the weight of public interest that forced the hands of the BRB into allowing the run to take place.

I was teaching in Stevenage and succeeded in persuading my headmaster that it would be in the best interests of the school railway society to be on Langley Bridge when the 'Scotsman' went through. Little did I know that the locomotive and the inspector on the footplate were to play an important part in my life, although it took a disagreement with the said headmaster and a spot of high dudgeon to bring it to pass!

The fortieth anniversary run was well covered by television and the newspapers. The BBC TV film must have been screened at least half a dozen times since the event took place – and it is refreshing to have the views of a man who was very involved with events on the day.

With George Harland as his assistant, Les Richards was totally responsible for the engine and for making the decision that brought about the success of the project. He and George shared the footplate work on an hour on/hour off basis. Les recalls how impressed he was with the acceleration of 4472 leaving King's Cross compared with the Deltic that left at the same time. 'We beat the Deltic into the tunnel by an engine and a couple of coaches, but when we came out of the other end the Deltic had beaten us.'

The engine performed quite well and the only thing that gave rise to anxiety was the water situation. 4472 was equipped with a second tender and George Harland was in favour of opening the valves between the two tenders early in the journey, but Les decided that this would not be done until absolutely necessary. 'We argued considerably,' continued Les, 'until in the finish I said to George that up to now I hadn't given him any definite instructions, but I was giving him one now – they stay shut.' Les contended that by keeping the valves closed they knew that they had a full tank of water and his decision was quite justified. At Scrooby troughs they picked up only 1,000 gallons because the level of water in the troughs was well below normal. The tender valves were then opened until Wiske Moor troughs where they had a good dip and the valves were then closed, and stayed closed until Morpeth when they were re-opened. Much to the consternation of those on the footplate, Luker troughs were virtually empty and they were unable to pick up any water. Les now had to decide whether or not the journey could continue non-stop, or if they should notify the signalman at Beale by using a pre-arranged 'water' whistle that water was required. A road tanker was waiting at Tweedmouth for such an emergency and on hearing the whistle the Beale signalman would advise Tweedmouth accordingly. Les takes up the story: 'I went through the tender and held my hand against the tank side – you can, if you have the experience, feel the flush of water on the tank. Well, I felt where the water was and estimated the amount of water and decided that we had sufficient to go.'

On the approach to Beale station, the driver noticed that there were several spectators very close to the edge of the platform and his warning

32. King's Cross, 1 May 1968. A3 Pacific 4472, 'Flying Scotsman', is about to depart for Edinburgh to commemorate the fortieth anniversary of the first non-stop run. Beside it, also awaiting departure with the 'Flying Scotsman' train, is Deltic 9021, 'Argyll and Sutherland Highlander'.

G R Mortimer

whistle was misinterpreted by the signalman. As a result, when the train reached Tweedmouth the signals indicated that it was being 'put inside' – main line to slow line – presumably for water. The vocal efforts of those on the footplate told the signalman that water was not required. Then came a breath-holding crawl through Berwick yard with the signal, to put the train back onto the main line, clearly visible – at danger. Fortunately, it was pulled off in time, the train was out onto the main line without stopping and it arrived in Edinburgh with about 900 gallons of water in the tender, and on time.

The success of the trip was due in no small measure to the way in which the driver worked the engine from Tweedmouth and conserved the water. Alan Pegler was much exercised and was in favour of trying to rush things. They were 15 minutes behind time at Berwick but Les would not permit any interference, such was his confidence in the driver coupled with his own knowledge of the route.

Les Richards retired from British Railways in 1969 since when he has devoted his time to 4472 and to Flying Scotsman Enterprises. This has involved two extended trips to the United States, one of seven months and the other of nine months, the latter ending in financial disaster for Alan Pegler and the impounding of the engine in San Francisco.

The circumstances surrounding the return of 4472 to this country are well documented elsewhere and since 1973 she has been owned by Bill McAlpine and operated by Flying Scotsman Enterprises, under the watchful eyes of George Hinchcliffe and Les Richards.

I have had the privilege and pleasure of working on 4472 with the FSE team. I've spent a night on the footplate, keeping the fire in and the water level correct, I've ridden on the engine on the main line, I've spent hours whilst on static display showing visitors over it, I've been sent between the frames to clean the inside gear and I've driven the engine. At all times Les Richards has explained, demonstrated and taught not only me but many enthusiastic volunteers and shared with us his encyclopaedic knowledge of the steam locomotive. He is more than a man of the LNER – he is a gentleman of the LNER.

4
Stratford

There exists between Stratford men and King's Cross men something akin to a love/hate relationship. The former are rather condescending in their references to King's Cross men being able to drive only in straight lines with little deviation either side of the East Coast main line. The King's Cross men are somewhat patronising in their references to East Anglian workings as 'glorified shunts'. One former King's Cross man remarked that the Stratford men are everywhere and he assured me that when Captain Scott reached the South Pole, he found a couple of Stratford men waiting for him.

Now had that been the case, then the Stratford men in question would undoubtedly have been contemporaries of Charles Francis, who joined the Great Eastern Railway as a cleaner in 1898. This was the time when James Holden was very much in charge of locomotive affairs and he made his mark in a variety of ways. He completely re-organised Stratford works with standardisation and ease of maintenance as his criteria and, when he became convinced that the bogie locomotive was here to stay, he introduced two distinct classes each of which has a place in locomotive history, but for very different reasons. The 4–4–0 Claud Hamilton class is considered by many to be the finest example of a 4–4–0 ever to appear on any British railway, and the 4–2–2 class was the last single driving

wheel locomotive to be introduced in this country.

As a cleaner, Charlie Francis worked on these locomotives at a time when locomotive cleaning meant precisely that. During the first two years he was a member of a gang working exclusively on tank engines, before graduating to express passenger engines. The cleaning gangs were required to clean five engines per shift and the cleaning included scouring the buffers, wiping the motion with tallow and then standing back whilst the drivers inspected the work. Charlie recalled that some drivers were reasonably easy to please, but that some would actually examine the backs of the spokes of the wheels and woe betide the cleaners if the spokes were dirty.

In 1902 after four years of this rather harsh regime, Charlie became a spare fireman in the goods link working a 10 hour day. He spent several months in the Peterborough link working freight and mineral trains between Temple Mills yard and Whitemoor yard and this included some lodging turns. At the time, his pay was 3s 9d ($18\frac{1}{2}$p) per day and with overtime he could earn as much as £2.00 per week.

One highlight of this period was the preparation of locomotive 1900 for the Paris Exhibition of 1910. Charlie was involved in the project and recalled the Great Eastern blue livery, lined out in red, the burnished buffers and motion and the copper-capped chimney.

P H Groom

33. Norwich (Thorpe) on 2 September 1955. B12/3 61547 leaves with a train for Cromer whilst D16/3 62540 approaches with a local train. Both classes of locomotive had their origins with the Great Eastern Railway and were modified by Gresley.

The backs of the spokes were given special attention! 1900 was 4–4–0 Claud Hamilton class engine, 'Claud Hamilton'. Named after the chairman of the GER, it was the prototype of the class and was introduced in 1900, but numbered out of sequence. It was one of only four GER engines to be named.

During the First World War, Charlie spent some time working on ambulance trains.

'We'd run light with, say, a Claud from Stratford to Liverpool Street,' he said, 'and be put alongside the road into platform 18. Eventually an ambulance train would come in, the engine would come off, we'd drop onto the train and not know where we were going until someone handed the driver a piece of blue paper. It might be Norwich, it might be Snaresbrook or it might be Whipps Cross.'

In 1919 and after 15 years as a fireman, Charlie became a driver and his pay was increased to 5s 6d (37½p) a day. He had been married for 10 years and he had a family of three children to

34. 62570, an example of the fourth type of variant of the D16/3, awaits departure time at Liverpool Street. This type of locomotive was a rebuild of the D16/2 but, as will be noted, the original footplating was retained.

support so, as he put it, the extra money came in useful.

The years between the wars saw Charlie involved in a variety of driving turns. He signed the road to Norwich, King's Lynn, Clacton, Bury St Edmunds and Lowestoft and spent some time in the goods link working, once again, Temple Mills to Peterborough via Ely, Cambridge and March.

'That trip,' he said, 'was a Sunday night regular – 100 empties down and 50 of coal coming back. I've known the time when we've been so late back that I've barely had three hours sleep before work. But I used to like the 2.50 a.m. paper train,' he went on, 'we were down to Norwich with her and back to Liverpool Street with the 8.22 a.m. We'd then come off the train, turn the engine, coal and oil her and work to Croydon via East London with the 11 o'clock.' For four of the years during this

42

P J Lynch

35. E4 2–4–0 62795 leaves Cambridge with a two-coach local train on 20 April 1953. These locomotives were designed by James Holden and introduced in 1891 and the author has fond memories of going down from Cambridge to Sudbury behind members of this class on several occasions.

period, Charlie worked the Ilford – Shenfield – Fairlop section over lines now operated by London Transport and he also worked some of the Essex branch lines, many of which have now disappeared. He remembered working to Buntingford, Dunmow, Witham and Maldon and on the Ipswich – Felixstowe branch, where a country-bred colleague taught him how to catch rabbits.

Conversation turned to the General Strike of 1926 and Charlie recalled an incident that both amused and exasperated him.

'I was by a water column at Stratford,' he said, 'when one of those volunteer chaps brought a loco in for water. Well, he couldn't stop at first then he couldn't start, then he couldn't stop again until in the end I said to him, "Here, you stop where you are and I'll move the column to you".'

The Second World War also had its share of incidents such as the train load of bombs that ran out of control on Brentwood bank. Charlie was of the opinion that the driver was unfamiliar with the road and misread the signals. He made

43

36. The down 'Norfolkman' leaves Ipswich behind Britannia class 4–6–2 70039, 'Sir Christopher Wren'.

a heavy brake application and it is assumed that a coupling broke, resulting in considerable damage to the track and serious disruption to train services.

He had a vivid recollection of working an 18 hour shift during the war as the result of a strike by some of the firemen at Stratford. One of them was disciplined for allegedly insulting a member of the ATS and when the company refused to re-instate him, some of his colleagues walked out. A message came through that a locomotive was required urgently at Liverpool Street, so Charlie had to act as fireman and he and his driver set off. The engine was in rough condition and it was reported as such at Liverpool Street, where it transpired that it was needed at Hertford. The crew had no option but to carry on because there just wasn't a replacement available. Passing through Ware the driver shut off steam and the little-end pin sheared, which knocked the front off one of the outside cylinders and the locomotive failed completely.

Eventually, a relief engine was sent from Broxbourne and the casualty was towed back to Liverpool Street. 'And,' said Charlie, 'I paid £3 10s 0d (£3.50) income tax that week.'

Charlie Francis retired from railway service in August 1946. He was a man of deeply religious convictions and a lifelong teetotaller and non-smoker. He died in October 1978 aged 97.

(Much of the above information was taken from a taped conversation between Charlie Francis and Frank Mayes recorded in 1970. I am grateful to Frank Mayes and to the family of the late Charlie Francis for allowing me access to the tape and for permission to transcribe it.)

One damp, Sunday lunchtime in August 1975 I was sitting in the cab of A4 60007, 'Sir Nigel Gresley', talking to two members of the A4 Society who were in charge of the engine. 60007 was one of a group of 10 preserved locomotives that were on exhibition at Darlington Bank Top station as part of the Rail 150 celebrations. I had

44

37. A view of Stratford MPD taken on 12 October 1957. Locomotives on shed include B1s, a J15, and various 0–6–2T and 0–6–0T.

38. King's Lynn MPD on 15 April 1947. The 'historic' collection of locomotives includes a D16 and a J15. Not quite so old is the Gresley K2/2.

the privilege of being in control of the exhibition for the week of its duration on behalf of Flying Scotsman Enterprises.

Typically, I suppose, and on cue, as the late Bishop Treacey cut the tape and declared the exhibition open it started to rain. I conducted the invited guests around the exhibits and this done, I sought refuge on 60007 – the lads had been sufficiently far-sighted to put the canopy in place between the cab roof and the tender and so had a dry footplate.

As a railway centre, Darlington has seen better days – the glory is indeed departed. Gone are North Road works, gone is Darlington shed and all that remains is a dmu stabling and servicing depot, which also serves as a signing-on point for drivers, about half a mile from the north end of the station.

'I've got this one in the cavalcade,' said a voice. I looked out of the cab window and there was a driver on his way to work. We invited him onto the footplate out of the rain, now falling relentlessly from a lowering, leaden sky and forming thousands of rivulets down the pristine, garter blue casing of 60007. He was joined by one of his colleagues who was also on his way to work and who, it transpired, was to be in charge of 4472, 'Flying Scotsman', in the cavalcade.

Had either of them, we enquired, driven 60007 or 4472 before? No they hadn't but they had driven engines of the same classes. 'The best A3 we ever had at Darlington was 36 [60036, "Colombo"],' asserted one. There was a pause, an incredulous pause. 'Rubbish,' retorted his mate, 'it couldn't hold a candle to 85 [60085, "Manna"].'

And then the argument started and they were still at it as they walked along the platform on their way to sign on. Those of us who were privy to the conversation were spellbound and it occurred to me some time afterwards that it should have been recorded.

In the event, over three years elapsed before I had the opportunity to tape a discussion with a group of drivers, and it was very much with the cab of 60007 in mind that I switched on my tape recorder in the presence of Alf Addison, Clem Britton and Charlie Fincham. The session was arranged, hosted and chaired by Frank Mayes and we started at 8.0 p.m. It ended at 12.30 a.m. when I ran out of cassettes.

Clem Britton, now Headquarters Traction Inspector York and based at Liverpool Street, opened the discussion.

'Every depot had its characters,' he said and recalling his days at Stratford he mentioned 'Chopper' Smith, 'Hot box' Furness and 'Chimney Wobbler' Cook. 'They always made sure that he (Cook) had a big, strapping fireman because if he heard of anyone passing, say, Shenfield in 27 minutes, he'd want to do it in 26. I remember relieving him at Liverpool Street on the first day that a new train ran from Yarmouth – he ran in with six hot boxes on a B17.'

One of Clem's regular drivers was something of an eccentric. They started as a team in the Parkeston link and Clem was a trifle nonplussed to discover that at the end of his second week with Bob he didn't have any wages. Bob had forgotten to send the necessary forms to the office and the footplatemen were only paid if the driver's daily returns – known locally as the ticket – were sent in.

'He was a big man,' said Clem, 'he'd push the regulator on a 1500 right over, take the lock nut off, push the regulator handle a bit further and then put the nut back.' And, with what must have been a masterly piece of understatement, described his driving as erratic.

'But above all he was a gentleman,' continued Clem, 'and he couldn't resist helping the ladies. He once came on the engine at Liverpool Street 13 minutes late and, without paying the slightest attention to anybody, off we went. We were

39. N7/5 69665 at Liverpool Street with an Enfield train on 30 April 1958. The tank side sheets and Westinghouse pump casing are immaculate but it seems that enthusiasm waned after the dome had been cleaned!

P J Lynch

first stop Chelmsford and I asked him where he'd been. It transpired that he'd assisted a lady off the train and then carried her bags to Broad Street. We ran into Parkeston only four minutes down.'

'Then there was Len Hay,' said Alf. 'He was on the footplate in Liverpool Street when a passenger asked if he should change for Norwich. Quick as a flash Len said, "No, you're all right dressed as you are."'

What was important so far as footplate relationships were concerned was, to quote Charlie Fincham, 'a sweet start to the day'. 'Put your driver in a good mood by arriving about 30 minutes earlier than he did.'

As might be expected, there were variations in the procedures at different depots. At Stratford firemen did not expect their drivers to take much part in disposal duties, whereas at Norwich it didn't even occur to the drivers that disposal was other than the fireman's affair. There were recognised and recognisable divisions of labour, and indeed of social position. In the Norwich messroom there were four tables – two for

40. B1 61361 in a rural setting, working a three-coach local train from Ipswich up Belstead Bank in the long hot summer of 1959.

drivers, one for firemen and one for cleaners. If a fireman went to the messroom and his table was full even though there might be a vacancy at the drivers' table, he wouldn't dare sit at it. On night shift if three drivers were short of a player to make up a game of solo they would wait until another driver came in, rather than ask a fireman to be the fourth player.

The three men agreed that there were few changes in working conditions before and during the war. Charlie Fincham considered himself fortunate to get a job on the railway in 1934 and he had to work as an office boy at Stratford until he was old enough to become a cleaner. His office boy hours are interesting: 9 a.m. – 6 p.m. six days a week and 9 a.m. – 1 p.m. Sundays for 15s (75p) per week. He then followed his father and grandfather onto the footplate and maintained that it was his father's influence that got him the job. He was sent to Ilford as a cleaner, but the outbreak of World War II and the consequent lack of manpower found him doing a variety of jobs from ashman to emptying coal trucks. He became a fireman in March 1941 after five years in the cleaners' grades and was compulsorily transferred to Southend, where he worked on goods trains to Goodmayes, Wickford and Southminster.

48

'We were using J39s – the old "knockjohns" – at that time,' he said, 'and they were powerful. Unlike the GE engines they didn't have wedges in the axle boxes and they were a bit top heavy. They used to develop a sort of vertical movement and many's the time I thought that we'd come off. I remember working the down Southend papers with a "knockjohn". Charlie Francis was my mate and we had a lightly loaded train. Well, she got into this bouncing motion and old Charlie told me to screw down the handbrake. Charlie was frightened but he didn't panic. I screwed the brake on and he opened her up and eventually she settled down. Soon after that one of them did bounce off the road and they were banned from that section.'

After three months at Southend, Charlie Fincham was transferred to Stratford and did a stint of shed shunting. There were about 200 locomotives based at Stratford at that time and shed work in the blackout was a complicated procedure.

This prompted other reminiscences of wartime. Because GE engines were equipped with Westinghouse brakes, drivers were asked to volunteer to drive American ambulance trains – take their engines and go anywhere in the country. In addition, the Stratford drivers' route knowledge was very extensive, some signing the road as far as Doncaster whilst some of the Southend men signed to Whitemoor via the Whickam triangle. Alf Addison recalled firing on the local goods between King's Lynn and Dereham and handling train loads of bombs. Charlie added that the Southminster branch trip at night could be 'hairy', because the Spitfire base at Rochford attracted attention from German bombers.

'I remember being fireman on the Romford pilot again with Charlie Francis,' went on Charlie, 'and the driver of the 8.12 a.m. Ipswich decided he wanted the pilot from Liverpool Street. Actually he was worried in case somebody else grabbed us. Anyway, we coupled up at Liverpool Street and this driver – he had a Claud by the way – said to my mate, "You're not shunting a few wagons in the yard now – we're first stop Chelmsford." Now this upset my mate and, to cut a long story short, they had to knock the Claud off at Chelmsford with a hot box on the tender.'

At about this time during the war and due to acute labour shortages, men were drafted from the mines to become firemen – a sort of Bevin boys in reverse. (For the benefit of younger readers Bevin boys were men of military service age who opted to work in the mines rather than go into the armed forces. The scheme was introduced by the then Minister of Labour, Ernest Bevin. Perhaps the most famous ex-Bevin boy is Eric Morecambe.) Also, at this time, it was not uncommon to have an armed guard on the footplate with troop trains and some goods trains. As might be expected this was known as 'riding shotgun'.

Turning to the lighter side of working in and around East Anglia, Alf told of the incident of the cockerels.

'Working the "Fenman" from Hunstanton to Lynn one morning we hit a flock of cockerels at Wotton. We came back from Lynn light engine so we stopped and me and my mate had four or five apiece. We put 'em in the tool box and when we eventually got back to Hunstanton I cleared the fire and put the blower on. We sat plucking these cockerels until we heard a shout from the shunter, "What you b———s doing up there?" When we had a look there's feathers cascading from the chimney and the depot's nearly covered.

'And talking about being covered,' he continued, 'I was on a docks job with a driver called Wiseman. There was an inspector at the docks who was both fiery and impatient. Well,

41. Liverpool Street on 1 August 1950. B17/6 61600, 'Sandringham', awaits departure. Is that the fireman showing signs of impatience? In the foreground B1 61121 simmers somnolently in the afternoon heat whilst just behind it the sun reflects from two grease-top hats as secrets are exchanged about the unidentified B1.

we were setting back very carefully with a train of empties when this inspector starts shouting to us to get a move on. We were on a "buck-jumper" and they were bad for picking up the water if you weren't careful. My mate opened her up and, sure enough, she primed and water came out of the chimney. As luck would have it we were under a footbridge and a deluge of sooty water hit the bridge, bounced off it and off the boiler and the inspector shot back into his office – he looked like a plum pudding.'

'I had a mate once,' said Charlie, 'who was a spiritualist. He stopped a train we were working and was gazing ahead. "Can't you see," he said,

50

42. Darlington, August 1975. Ivatt 4MT 43106 with K1 2005 and A4, 'Sir Nigel Gresley', on exhibition at Bank Top Station as part of the Rail 150 celebrations.

"a legion of Roman soldiers crossing the track?" He used to chalk a line on the centre of the cab floor and we had to keep to our own halves.'

Continuing as it were in lighter vein, Clem recalled a day that he isn't likely to forget. It was his driver's birthday and they were on nights. At one minute past midnight the event was marked and they continued with a K3 on a goods train towards Cambridge. 'Going through Audley End,' said Clem, 'I happened to glance back and saw a lot of sparks. I checked the firebars – no problems there – and so we carried on. At Cambridge we were relieved and the guard came down in a right state to tell us that we'd a wagon with one wheel riding on a brake block – all the way from Audley End. Out came the carriage and wagon boys and the wagon had to be lifted. Now my mate didn't worry about any-thing and as we were due for relief didn't consider that it was his problem.

'We had our meal break and whilst we were in the cabin we had a phone call to tell us that there'd been a loco failure at Audley End. It was decided that the first train up would go into Whittlesford sidings, engine off and forward to Audley to pick up the failure and that the second train up would go into Whittlesford to pick up the first train. Now we were the second train and at Whittlesford the guard decides on how the shunt should be done. He gave us permission to pass the signal and my mate opens up. Bang – six wheels off the road – the guard had forgotten about the points. We came back to Stratford on the cushions and booked off. We booked on again that night, still my mate's birthday re-member, and found that the K3 was back in the

51

depot. We had to prep her and as she was facing the wrong way my mate put her onto the turntable. We spun the table but it stopped about 2 inches short and another fireman walking past shouted to my mate to warn him. He thought it was me shouting to him and off he sets. Bang – she's on the floor again. He got off the footplate, looked at the engine and said, "I'll be bloody glad when my birthday's over." I had a happy time with old Ted,' Clem continued, 'he wasn't the best driver in the world but he was a jolly good mate. He knew every lineside pub between Liverpool Street and Cambridge.'

One problem that has faced the GE section of the former LNER since the turn of the century has been the volume of commuter traffic with which it has had to cope. Before the lines were electrified various types of steam traction were tried including Holden's monstrous 'Decapod', an 0–10–0 which was built to prove that a steam locomotive could accelerate a commuter train at the same rate as could an electric locomotive. Perhaps the most successful steam type used on the Liverpool Street commuter trains was the N7, a design originally introduced by A. J. Hill in 1914 and perpetuated by Gresley until 1928. The allocation of both men and machines to the 'Jazz' was very carefully organised and the links structure at Stratford was far more complex than at other depots. The commuter services – the Jazz – were arranged as follows:

N7a link. Bishops Stortford
N7b. Chelmsford
N7c. Hertford – Shenfield
N7d. Epping – Ongar – Fenchurch Street
Intermingled with the latter were turns to Woodford, Hainault and London to London via Ilford and Fairlop or via Leytonstone and Woodford. In addition the N7s worked to Audley End and to Southend on Sundays.

It is interesting to note that these links were named after the locomotives that worked them and that each link had twenty-four sets of them.

Following the 'Jazz' links came the goods links and then the normal sort of progression – a plod through the links to main line passenger work. The GE section had its share of lodging turns and some of the men from March depot lodged in London until the 1950s. Lodging turns were discontinued during the war and the company wanted to re-introduce them when the war ended but met with resistance from the unions. Charlie Fincham said that his father told him that by not lodging he didn't know what he was missing which proves that lodging turns were not all unpopular!

Extended turns replaced lodging turns to some extent. In this case, a crew might work an excursion train, say, to Southend on a Sunday and have a break of about six hours before returning to Liverpool Street.

As Clem, Charlie and Alf reflected on their various progressions through the links until the time that they became drivers, Alf observed that he sometimes despaired of some of his firemen ever being able to drive properly. 'And yet,' he said, 'it was surprising what six months on the road after passing out as a driver could do.'

They all worked 'day and day' about with their firemen and they agreed that their mates never took this for granted. On this point Frank Mayes disagreed: 'I had one mate,' he said, 'who assumed that he was going to drive. "You like firing these don't you Frank," he said to me at the beginning of one shift. "Yes," I said, "and I like to drive 'em – move over."'

Charlie recalled a fireman that he worked with who had been a driver and who had for some reason been demoted. They were due to take a partially fitted goods train and the fireman went to the foreman to find out which locomotive they had for the trip. He came back with the news that they had a very run-down B1. Charlie himself then went to the foreman to protest,

43. A3 Pacific 60036, 'Colombo', at Darlington MPD on 2 May 1964. This locomotive was station pilot at Darlington until the depot closed.

particularly in view of the fact that there was a depot full of diesels. It transpired that the fireman was, in fact, somewhat maliciously pulling Charlie's leg and that they had a diesel. When tackled about it he remarked, 'You bloody boy drivers would have your heart in your boots at the prospect of a steamer.'

'Two or three days later,' Charlie continued, 'I spotted a beaten up WD that had been running about Ripple Lane – 90551 and she was a cab ranker if ever there was one. I went to see the foreman and I asked for the WD. He told me that no one would take her. I said that I would. To cut a long story short, I bashed the living daylights out of her and by the time that we got to the end of the trip the fireman wasn't speaking – he couldn't. It took him all his time to put on the tender handbrake. Anyway, after that we were the best of friends.'

Clem's incident did not, however, have the same happy ending. He was driving by the time that he was 28 and, although he was unaware of the fact, his fireman was aged 35. They worked day and day about and on one occasion, when it was Clem's turn to fire, the guard came to the engine to give details of the train to the driver.

53

Now the guard didn't know about the day and day about arrangement and when the 'driver' asked for the information the guard replies, rather acidly, 'Can't see I should tell you, boy.' There was something of a scene on the footplate and it wasn't helped when the fireman discovered that he had been firing for a driver seven years his junior.

'And from that day,' said Clem, 'he would never help with disposal. He did himself out of an hour's overtime at the end of the shift, because he couldn't accept that I was a driver at 28 and he was still firing at 35, even though I'd joined the company before he did.'

I managed to turn the conversation towards the different types of locomotives on which Alf, Charlie and Clem had worked and asked them to talk about their favourites. Clem maintained that the 'Britannias' were the best that he had worked on.

'My 39 [70039, "Sir Christopher Wren"] would climb trees, but of course I was working with a good mate. I didn't like the "Raggys" – the K1s – and I can't really tell you why. The Clauds were all right and the 2800s weren't too bad and a Norwich B1 was as good as anything. As a fireman, if I got a Norwich B1, I knew that I was in for a good trip.'

The L1s were discussed and opinions differed. Clem said that they did some good work on the Chelmsford and Southend runs, and that he'd been down to King's Lynn from Liverpool Street without having to take water. Frank Mayes expressed surprise at this, and said that it was the experience of some of the King's Cross men that the L1s did not run well bunker first

and on an all-stations to Cambridge trip, if Shepreth Junction was reached with water still on the tap, they'd done very well.

The three then ganged up on Frank and asked him which was his favourite engine. 'Well,' he replied, 'I used to say at King's Cross that if I had to choose between my wife and number 29 [A4 60029, "Woodcock"] my wife wouldn't have a look in.'

The discussion then centred around the steaming and riding qualities of various types and the relative merits of different depots, so far as maintenance was concerned. Charlie brought a down to earth note into the conversation when he said that he always went for creature comforts in the cab. 'The outstanding ones as far as I'm concerned were the J39s,' he said. 'They were comfortable, had good visibility, were warm in winter and cool in summer.'

Alf said that in his experience 8783 the Royal Claud was an outstanding engine. It was always well maintained and in pristine condition. 'As soon as we ran into the loco at Lynn,' he said, 'the cleaners were out polishing the rings around the smokebox and boiler and at the first sign of a wisp of steam, glands and packing were replaced. The cab was mahogany lined and the seats were varnished. It was marvellous having that engine.'

And so both time and recording tape ran out. The evening's entertainment – and how else could it be described – had taken us all over the Great Eastern section and deep into East Anglia, now virtually isolated so far as railways are concerned.

5 Gateshead

'It's all right these silly b———s saying that steam is marvellous – steam is marvellous as a toy to play with, but if you have to make your bread and butter with it, it's bloody hard work. And there's no comparison about the ease a diesel does it and a steam engine. And it's a lot of bull about diesels doing it themselves – you've got to know what you're doing and there's a lot to know.'

George Jennings, quoted verbatim, joined the LNER as a cleaner at Gateshead shed in February 1944. Within two weeks and at the age of 16 he was passed for firing, although he didn't become a fireman, officially, until 1948 and he became a driver in 1959.

As has already been noted, promotion in the footplate grades was always a slow process with seniority being jealously guarded and taking precedence over competence, but it seems that in the North-East it was even slower than normal. There is an instance of a fireman at Tweedmouth shed reaching retiring age, 65, and retiring as a fireman, and George said that it was not uncommon for depots such as Tweedmouth and Whitby having firemen aged 55 to 60. Because of the dismal promotion prospects there was some migration to other depots, particularly in the South, but it was not until the North Eastern and Eastern regions of BR were amalgamated that the North Eastern men were eligible to apply to King's Cross. George spent 26 years at Gateshead depot before transferring to Tyne Yard and although he considered moving to King's Cross, certain domestic problems kept him in the North-East. He was, at the time, firing on the London turns and a move to the 'Cross' might have meant a loss in earnings. In any case, so far as he was concerned, Gateshead was *the* depot on the Eastern and far more prestigious than King's Cross. (The author has no desire to enter into correspondence on this point!) At that particular time Gateshead had an across-the-board allocation of locomotives including eight A4s, the numbers and names of which George still recalls. 'There was 1, 2, 5, 16, 18, 19, 20 and 23,' he said [60001, 60002, 60005 and so on]. 'Number one, Ronnie Matthews, was a poor engine, a bad steamer; but number five, Charlie Newton, one of the four originally fitted with a double blastpipe, was a great engine – couldn't keep her quiet. Of course, we had A3s and Peppercorn A1s – "Borderer" and "Bon Accord" were my regular engines on the London trips – and I reckon that the A3s fitted with double blastpipes were as good in the last few years of their working lives as anything that we ever had, they were marvellous. Mind you, they had to put the smoke deflectors on them to keep the exhaust out of the cabs, but after that – marvellous. That was one of the difficulties with the blue 'uns [A4s]. The double blastpipes caused soft exhaust and it drifted back along the casing and filled the cab. As a result the drivers would pull 'em up to 10 per cent cut-off and work them harder.'

Other types that were remembered were V1s, V2s, V3s, J72s, J73s, N10s and former NER 4–6–0s, classified as B16s. Gateshead also had several B1s, numbers 61011, 61012, 61013 and 61014 being delivered new to Gateshead for work on the Carlisle run and replacing the Hunt class (D49). These were rough riding engines and those fitted with poppet valves (D49/1) were difficult to handle. Instead of an infinitely variable cut-off, it was stepped up or down 10 per cent at a time. According to George they did their best work whilst running downhill in mid-gear – this allowed the valves to fall away from their faces and the engines were unrestricted. 'Of course,' he continued, 'the B1s would roughen up very quickly. They never seemed to get the balancing of the wheels right so we adopted the Midland practice of coasting in mid-gear. Normally, we'd coast with the regulator closed and 25 per cent cut off. This meant that the snifting valve worked and that the superheater elements were kept cool. If we put her into mid-gear, however, the compression created in the cylinders would smooth out the knocks and bangs. I tell you that a smooth ride on a B1 was quite exceptional. As for the big Thompsons they were bloody awful and the Peppercorns weren't much better.'

Going back to his early days, George outlined the links structure, which, as might be expected, followed the established pattern, common to other depots.

1st link. Stabling and preparation link.

2nd link. Relief link – pick up engine and train at Newcastle Central – train to Heaton for servicing and the engine to the depot. There was, of course, the reverse working.

Pilot link. Yard work and container traffic.

Local goods link. Newport (Teesside) and back.

Local passenger link. Workings to Sunderland and Middlesbrough.

Spare link. Working as required.

Main line link. Known locally as the 'groups': goods and passenger to Edinburgh, Leeds, Carlisle and Grantham.

Top link. Volunteer link – so called because whilst working in this link was compulsory for firemen it was voluntary for drivers. Most of the Gateshead – King's Cross turns in this link were night shift turns and were double homes or lodging turns. All trains that ran between 00.01 and 02.00 were known locally as midnights and George said that he had recorded 1,004 turns in the top link.

George talked of experiences as a 16-year-old fireman and commented on the attitudes of various drivers towards an inexperienced fireman. He recalled being booked on to fire a Darlington goods train and the driver refusing to take him and insisting that the spare link fireman should go. It so happened that later in the same shift, the fireman rostered to the 4.15 p.m. Edinburgh train didn't report for work and George had his first taste of firing an A4.

He also had his first experience of firing to his father when they were rostered to an Edinburgh excursion, although father-son and brother-brother combinations on the footplate were avoided as far as possible. This was not through any considerations of individual psychology or clashes of temperament, but the much more practical consideration that in the event of an accident one family would lose two male members. There were occasions when this could not be avoided and George's first trip with his father was a rough one. 'He was at me all the way,' said George, 'and eventually we had a barney. When we got back I got off the engine and threatened to tell mother when I got home. After that he was all right.'

In George's opinion a good driver was one

who was, first and foremost, a good mate. 'I remember booking on at 4.45 a.m. on one Sunday to work the Low Fell pilot. We had a J39 and as I walked to the engine the driver caught me up and said that he didn't allow smoking, swearing or spitting on his engine, that I must walk 10 yards behind him and only breathe when he gave permission. We were snowed up on one occasion,' he continued, 'and as there was little chance of moving we sheeted up the cab – we had an N10 at the time – and then the driver closed both gauge cocks and deliberately smashed the gauge glasses. He handed me two new ones and a spanner and told me to change them, saying that it would be good practice for me. He was right!

'Ay,' he continued, 'and talking about gauge glasses we were just on Wiske Moor troughs with 533 [A1 60533, "Happy Knight"] when there was a hell of a bang and both of 'em went. I was showered in broken glass and had injuries to my mouth and tongue. That was the day before I started my holidays. But broken glass and blood didn't matter, the gauge glasses had to be replaced.

'I had another driver,' he went on, 'who was a right villain. Mind he was a good engineman but invariably the worse for drink. We worked round the coast and had a three minute stop for water at Stockton. He was off the engine, disappeared for a pint but we were away on time.'

Going back to the training of firemen and the attitude of drivers George related his first driving experience. He was firing to a driver called Matty Agar and they were rostered to the 'Flying Scotsman' to Grantham and back from Grantham with the 'Talisman'.

'We'd just got onto the King Edward bridge when Matty said that as he was putting on weight he was going to fire and that I was to be the driver. He fired each way and at the time that

was the longest single turn in the country – 326 miles for a day's work.'

Gateshead provided the enginemen with a wide variety of workings. There were several freight and parcels turns, one of which was a pick up job to York via the coast route – Sunderland, Hartlepool, Stockton, Eaglescliffe, Thirsk, Northallerton and on to York. It was a six hour trip to York and then back to Newcastle on the 'Heart of Midlothian'. The opposite working involved taking the 'second Scotsman' from Newcastle to York 'as fast as you could turn a wheel', relief at York, a very quick cup of tea and then back to Newcastle with a main line parcels train. This could take six or seven hours with protracted stops at Thirsk, Northallerton and Darlington. As platform 8 at Newcastle Central was the only platform that could accommodate parcels trains, delays here were frequent and on one occasion George and his mate were waiting for some hours at Low Fell before they could get into Central Station.

At the end of the war George Jennings was in the local passenger link. This was worked by six sets of men working two shifts, a 'front' shift and a 'back' shift. The crews had their own engines and by mutual agreement the early turn, or front shift men, did the preparation and oiling of the engines. A typical routine was engine to Scotswood Bridge to pick up the train then work a stopping train from Newcastle Central to Hartlepool. Here the train would be shunted, the engine would run round and the crew would have a meal break. This would be followed by a stopping train to Sunderland then all stations to South Shields, back to Sunderland, back to Newcastle Central and book off.

Soon after the war came nationalisation and whilst not wishing to introduce a political note, honesty compels me to record that George was less than enthusiastic about it. 'It was,' he said,

44. B16/3 4–6–0 61472 at Gateshead MPD on 23 July 1960. The B16/3 was a Thompson rebuild of a Raven 4–6–0 classified B16/1 by the LNER. The three 'men of the LNER' might well be reflecting on the improvement that Thompson made by replacing the Stephenson valve gear with Walschaerts.

'viewed by many North Eastern and Eastern men as Midlandisation and paralysation. Many little things went or were changed. We lost our own particular style of overalls and the grease top cap was introduced. Mind, if the LNER hadn't been nationalised it would have gone under in 1948 as a result of the flash floods and washouts – it couldn't possibly have had the resources to cope with the engineering works.'

Promotion through the links after the war was steady and progressive and by the mid-fifties George was firing regularly on the London turns. As already mentioned, many of Gates-head's important turns were night trips to King's Cross with a veritable procession of trains leaving between midnight and 02.00. The crews would lodge in hostels at either Kentish Town or St Pancras and then work back on one of the following: 7.30 p.m. (the down 'Aberdonian'), 8.00 p.m., 10.15 p.m. or the 10.35 p.m. If a driver and fireman were rostered to the 1.00 a.m. Newcastle – King's Cross, then they could have the statutory minimum of nine hours off duty and sign on for their return working in the early evening, thus having signed on for work twice on the same day. This

58

was not the case, however, with the 11.14 p.m. up mail train. The arrangements here were that the crew returned to Newcastle with the 3.00 p.m. next day, but the mail was subjected to long delays and it was not always possible for the men to have their nine hours off duty. In this event there was some re-arrangement of the schedules and the men worked the 'Talisman'. George said that on one or two occasions this wasn't possible and he and his mate returned to Newcastle as passengers. He went on to say that the up 'Talisman' was one of his favourite turns. For this working he signed on at 5.00 p.m., left Newcastle Central at 6.00 p.m. and arrived in King's Cross at 10.40 p.m. Here they would be relieved and go to the hostel at Kentish Town. George said that he enjoyed staying there – it was a very good place – but the hostel at the back of St Pancras station he described as 'a hacky, workhouse type' ('hacky' is a Tyneside word meaning 'grotty').

George's memory for incidents, accidents and happenings was remarkably clear and as during his main line firing days, 60155 (A1, 'Borderer') was his regular engine and not surprisingly it figures in some of these incidents.

'We'd just got our nose out of Gasworks Tunnel when a big tube went,' he said, 'luckily the firehole door was shut and by the time that we got into the platform the fire was out. What a bang. There was a roar of steam, water, dust and muck – you couldn't see anything. Anyway my mate, "Schoolboy" Parker, got her down to the buffers and there was no damage apart from the engine. On another occasion,' he continued, 'I was going to London with a driver called Kipling and we'd just got to Newark when I noticed a lot of sparks at my side. We stopped and examined but couldn't see anything so we continued on to London. When we got in there was a reception committee waiting for us and we were ordered not to move the engine until it had been examined. They'd found a driving spring, a lump of rod on the track and we only had one bolt in the middle big end. The spring had broken, come off and hit a sleeper and bounced back causing the damage – we'd done 120 miles like that.

'Then there was 964,' he went on [V2 60964]. 'We were coming back from York and there was such a bloody bang. We were coasting at the time so my mate opens up and we carried on. What had happened was that the bolt holding the leading crankpin had snapped, the rod came off and bent the motion bars but it went back on again. We managed to get to the depot but as soon as my mate tried to move her in reverse then everything jammed up and the rod had to be cut off with an acetylene torch.

'I was going to Edinburgh one day with "Durham School" [V2 60860] and we had a spot of bother with the left big end bearing – it ran hot. The train stopped at Dunbar and just as we were approaching the station, where there's a 10 mph slack over the crossover, the bush broke up and came out of the rod. As the rod went forward it knocked out the front cover of the cylinder and as it came back it did the same – fetched the whole lot down.'

Warming to his theme George continued with the tale of 60123 A1, 'H. A. Ivatt'.

'We had 123 on the 10.15 back from London,' he said. 'Now it had been laid up at King's Cross for some time and nobody seemed to know much about it. Anyway, we had it and on the way back and doing about 90 she began to lose bits – we lost crankpins, rods, footplating, the lot.' One of his colleagues had a similar experience when his engine shed a bush from one of the left-hand side coupling rods. As luck would have it, he actually saw it go and, showing great presence of mind, he advanced the cut-off to 10 per cent and 'whipped her up'. In so doing he kept the rod floating and prevented serious damage. George said that in his 26 years at Gateshead he reckoned that they averaged one serious incident a year.

But to my mind the Guy Fawkes night affair was potentially the most serious and at the same time, perhaps, the most hilarious – let George tell it himself.

'I was firing on the local goods,' he said, 'and we used to get a load from Park Lane to Durham goods, shunting at Fencehouses and sometimes down to the ammunition factory and shunt there. Then we'd go to Belmont Junction and then down to Durham goods. Now there'd been a landslip and the line ran about 100 feet above the river and we had a 5 mph slack on this section. We had a J39 on this particular night which was foggy and miserable and the kids had been out collecting old sleepers for the bonfires. We had to wait at Belmont for about an hour and as we came back over the 5 mph section it was inky black – not a light to be seen anywhere. We had about 15 on and we'd just passed the landslip and were doing about 6 or 7 mph when the engine reared up and started to go sideways. I immediately thought that the kids had put sleepers on the line and grabbed my lamp out of the locker. My mate jumped off the engine straight onto the back of a cow. What had happened was that 30 odd cows had got out of Willington and wandered through the centre of Durham City and onto the line. There was one trapped under the engine and we'd cut two or three in half and they'd put the engine off the road. In fact, the track was in such a bad state that we'd come off the road and back on again. We had one jammed under the cylinders and the ashpan was full of cow. My mate got off the back of one and onto the footplate – "Geordie, there's a bull." It was terrible at the time, there was bloody cows all over. I said to Joe Hackett, my mate, that he should try to ease back off the one we'd trapped, which we did, and that we

should get a vet. By this time the guard and I decided to go to Belmont for assistance. We set off up the track with one of the cows running in front of us. Suddenly it stopped, turned round and had a go at us and we had to climb the fence into the field. We got to the box and eventually a vet arrived and destroyed those that were badly injured. We'd killed seven and were delayed from about 6.30 p.m. to 11 o'clock. They had to get a tractor from the farm to move the one that we'd killed with the cylinders.

'A few days later we had to put in a report. My mate started to fill it in. He started it with, "We were proceeding from Durham goods to Belmont and we ran into a flock of cows." I pointed out to him that flock was for sheep and it should be a herd of cows. But he wasn't having that; "A flock sounds more," he said and that went in his report.'

Going back to post-nationalisation and the import of 'foreign' engines into Gateshead, George and his mate were on a local passenger job with an Ivatt 2–6–0, 43055. They were standing in Heaton sidings and were having some trouble with the injectors. While trying to rectify the problem the wooden floor of the cab gave way and George disappeared up to his arm-pits. Shaken, but otherwise unhurt, he was hauled out by his mate and they discovered that the cab floor was made of ordinary tongued and grooved boarding. It so happened that George's driver was the union representative and as a result of this incident, modifications were made to the cab floors of the Ivatt engines.

'Of course,' he said, 'the cab floors on our engines, the V2s, A3s and A4s was made of 1½-inch cross-grained oak. It would last a thousand years – unless,' he added as an after-thought, 'some silly b——— set fire to it.'

Before leaving his steam days to reflect on his diesel experiences, George recalled what was probably the outstanding run of his career. The

45. Queuing for water at Gateshead on 26 August 1954. A3 Pacific 60036, 'Colombo', waits patiently behind A8 4–6–2T 69871, the driver of which contemplates the scene whilst his mate busies himself with the oilcan.

date is firmly etched in his mind (2 January 1961), as is the train (the up 'Talisman') and the engine (A4 60010, 'Dominion of Canada'). At the time, the 'Talisman' ran non-stop from Newcastle to King's Cross on very tight timings. On this particular occasion, the engine working the train from Edinburgh failed and in consequence departure from Newcastle was at 6.58 p.m. instead of 6.15 p.m. Despite this, the train arrived at King's Cross at 10.28 p.m. and had had two out of course delays, one at York and one at Grantham, both signal checks. From

leaving Grantham, a dead stop at the end of the platform, to passing Peterborough, a distance of 29 miles, the time taken was 22 minutes. As luck would have it, the late Cecil J. Allen was a passenger on the train and he said that a speed of 120 mph was reached at Essendine. In any event, the run goes down as the fastest steam timing between Newcastle and King's Cross.

George Jennings's diesel days were not without incident. He trained on all types from dmu's and Claytons to Deltics. In view of the fact that the

61

Deltics are, at the time of writing, being relegated to secondary duties, will be phased out in the forseeable future and are becoming the objects of a cult, his comments and experiences will not be inappropriate. In his opinion, whilst all members of the class were excellent machines, he had no hesitation in selecting number 21 as the most outstanding. To avoid confusion, 21 was originally D9021 and was named 'Argyll and Sutherland Highlander'. It was the last of the class to be delivered and had, according to George, some minor modifications to the electrics that gave it an advantage over the rest of the class. D9021 became 9021 and when renumbering took place it became 55021 and 'St Paddy', originally D9001, became 55001.

In discussing number 21 a sombre note crept into the conversation. George had worked it down to Edinburgh with the 'Night Scotsman' and was returning to Newcastle as second man with the up 'Flying Scotsman'. As they came round the curve between St Germans and Long-niddry there was a man standing with one foot on the track. He ignored warning blasts from the horns and with the Deltic travelling at 75 mph and only two engine lengths away he stepped in front. The impact bent the coupling into a figure of eight shape, forced the hook back against the buffer beam, shattered the fibre glass thistle and wings emblem carried on the front of the cab and at the same time snapped the steel bar that supported it.

Less harrowing but perhaps more serious was the accident involving a mineral train. There was a working from Pontop Colliery with a load of 19x 21-ton wagons plus a brake van hauled by a type 3 diesel. The train called at Pelaw where the load was reduced to 10 wagons, the maximum permitted up to Consett. On this occasion, George took the train past Tyne Yard where they ran into signals trouble – there was a fault on the colour lights and the signals were at caution through to Pelaw. The signalman at Pelaw was unable to pull off his signals and George's second man, observing rule 55, got off the engine and 'phoned the box. Permission was given to pass the signal at danger, go into the yard and reduce the load before going on to Consett. George gently eased the engine forward and his mate went ahead with his hand-lamp and checked that the points were set correctly. When they reached the signal-box George applied more power and the engine jumped forward. He then realised that some-thing was wrong, and on checking discovered that he had lost the train – all that remained was one wagon. Eighteen wagons and the brake van were 'away down the bank' and it was 1,200 yards to the catch points. Of the 18 wagons, 17 were fitted with roller bearings and eleven of them were derailed at the points. The remainder carried on across the main line, just missing a passenger train, demolishing a control box in the process and effectively putting all colour lights from Ferryhill to Newcastle out of action. An enquiry revealed that a defective drawbar on one of the wagons was responsible for the mishap, and one outcome was the re-siting of the catch points about 150 yards nearer to the signal box.

George had no hesitation in choosing between steam and diesel traction with the few well-chosen words that opened this section. He comes from a long line of railwaymen and is, in fact, able to assert that there has been a Jennings on the railway in the North-East since the days of the Stockton and Darlington railway. He certainly had no illusions about the job, about the conditions and about some of the so-called improvements. His comments and observations were clear, concise and very objective. He broke with the family tradition of 'service until retire-ment' and I fancy that the Eastern region of BR has lost a good engineman.

6

The Dales, the West Riding and Newcastle upon Tyne

It cannot have escaped notice that several of the men who have provided the research material for this book – and for the others in the series – became railwaymen by accident. The railway provided the only chance of a job in the area in which they lived; redundancy from a chosen job forced some men to accept all that the labour exchange could offer. Despite this rather dubious start, all of them formed for themselves a career structure and one or two of them having reached the top in that branch of the work in which they found themselves.

Bob Tait is no exception in the context of responsibility. He reached the zenith of his career when he was appointed Assistant Stationmaster at Newcastle upon Tyne Central. Now this was no accident. He resolved to become a stationmaster before he left school and, furthermore, he resolved to be in charge of a station that required the stationmaster to wear a top hat on special occasions. With a note of regret in his voice he admitted that he failed, by the proverbial whisker, to make the top hat. Fate conspired against him and stationmasters and top hats were phased out whilst he was ASM at Newcastle.

In common with many of his contemporaries Bob came from a railway family and it was assumed that he too would follow a railway career. This assumption was accurate but not in the way that his family intended. His father was a plater and his brother a blacksmith, both employed on locomotive construction at North Road works, Darlington. Young Bob was destined to join them as a pattern maker but he thought otherwise. His interests lay in the operating side of railways and his ambition was to become a stationmaster. Any family objections were overcome and Bob Tait joined the LNER in 1939 as a lad number taker at Heighington, a station on the Darlington – Bishop Auckland branch. Judging from the 1939 Bradshaw there would be plenty to keep a lad number taker occupied – the timetable shows that 27 passenger trains per day stopped at Heighington. In addition, there would be extensive goods traffic not only from the South Durham coalfield but also from Shildon works

46. Newcastle Central, 27 August 1954. G5 0—4—4T 67230 on empty stock duty whilst D49/2 4—4—0 62771, 'The Rufford', waits with an up local train.

and from the agricultural regions of upper Weardale.

The outbreak of war in 1939 increased traffic through Heighington and brought about an up-grading in the status of the station. This was due to the building of an ordnance factory at Aycliffe and the construction of a spur to connect it with the branch. The first step on Bob Tait's promotional ladder came in 1941 when he transferred to the District Superintendent's office at Darlington as a junior clerk. Then came the inevitable interruption for war service and Bob returned from the Royal Navy to the LNER in 1946 to discover that jobs in the clerical grades were not easy to obtain. Determined to get back on the course that would lead to a station-mastership, he took the first job that was offered and became a motor driver at Darlington having worked for a time in the parcels office. The difficulty facing Bob was that he did not have an official clerical post to reclaim, as the position that he occupied in the District Superintendent's

64

47. J72 0–6–0T 68723, in immaculate condition, goes about its business as Newcastle Central station pilot in July 1961.

office had disappeared during the war. Eventually, a clerical vacancy arose at Scorton on the Darlington – Richmond branch and Bob's application was successful. He worked there for over a year and then moved to Catterick Bridge.

During his time there he learned signalling theory and took the necessary examination at the end of 1952. This was successful and was followed quickly by a very important move up the ladder when he was appointed stationmaster at Moulton on the Richmond branch. Here he was responsible for a staff consisting of two porter/signalmen, four category B crossing keepers and two each of category A and C. The distinction between the grades was based upon the hours worked and the conditions of service.

In most cases, the crossing keepers were appointed from the ranks of the men who had, through accident or illness, been down-graded. A crossing keeper's house was provided and the category B man was required to work a 12 hour day six days per week. As conditions improved, they were given one day off each week and an additional day per month known as 'market day'. The duties were not too onerous, merely opening and closing the crossing gates as required. The category A keepers worked a four-hour day six days a week and usually the category A keeper was the wife of the category B keeper. Thus the crossing was manned (or womanned?) for 16 hours a day. The category C keeper worked an eight hour day and if, as often

Ian S Carr

48. A3 Pacific 60096, 'Papyrus', arrives at Newcastle with the up 'Heart of Midlothian' on 9 April 1960.

happened on branch lines, there were two cross-ings very near to each other then one category C man would cover both, ostensibly being on duty for four hours at each. The exigences of the service up and down the Richmond branch at that time required the station to be open 20 hours a day and this meant that during a two hour period in the early afternoons, the stationmaster was on duty without any assistance.

'During that time,' said Bob, 'you did every-thing that was required to be done. You were signalman, porter and everybody else.' He recalled that there was regular coal traffic and, surprisingly, there was steady traffic in Clydes-dale horses between a breeder in Moulton and one in Newton Stewart in Scotland. In addition, there was some general livestock traffic – he described the goods traffic as 'steady but nothing dramatic'. Which contrasted markedly with Bob's next 'incumbency' – Holmfirth.

He stayed at Moulton until 1956 when he left the rural environment of the Richmond branch for the 'dark satanic mills' of what was then the West Riding, an area in which I not only spent my formative years but in which was fostered my love of railways.

66

49. A cold night in January 1960. A3 Pacific 60102, 'Sir Frederick Banbury', and crew obligingly pose for the camera at Newcastle Central shortly before leaving with the 22.25 to King's Cross.

Holmfirth is situated on the eastern edge of the Pennines, south of Huddersfield and west of Barnsley. When Bob took over responsibility for the station there was a heavy volume of freight traffic, much of it centred around the woollen industry. Raw wool and chemicals associated with its processing were handled inward and the finished cloth was handled outward. There was also an engineering works that specialised in the production of pulleys and overhead line shafts for the engineering industry. As modernisation overtook the industry and as plant and machinery became independently powered by electric motors, the Holmfirth concern gradually reduced its output until it closed and put a nail in the branch line's coffin. There was, in Bob's opinion, indecent haste in closing the branches in and around Holmfirth. Apart from the reduction in freight traffic, passenger services were withdrawn but not before a triple set dmu was tried on the branch to investigate whether or not it could cope with the gradients. This trial was abortive, however, and within three months of notices being posted, passenger services had gone. A gradual recession set in and Bob was transferred to Clayton West and with his family he lived in the station house at Shepley. From Clayton West Bob could go down the branches as required to Holmfirth, Meltham or Penistone. There was some commuter traffic with passenger trains mornings, evenings and on Saturday lunchtimes, but the bulk of Bob's work was concerned with freight traffic – coal and carpets.

67

50. Harrogate – a grubby D49/3 4–4–0 62738, 'The Zetland', stands at the head of a local passenger train of somewhat mixed stock. The signal is 'off', the blower is on and the safety valves are lifting. A 1.55 p.m. departure perhaps?

'It was,' said Bob, 'perhaps the last place in the North-East for training clerical staff. You could get a young person to come as a clerk and teach them a lot of the fast-disappearing aspects of railway work – freight sundries, freight full-loads, how to deal with coal, passengers, passenger parcels and more particularly traffic to the continent – it was that kind of place.

'The small branch line station was part of the community and people took an interest in it,' he continued, 'they would offer to help because they had the feeling of belonging.'

He cited the prizes that used to be offered for cleanliness and tidiness and for the best garden along the branch as incentives for the staff to take an interest in *their* station. Following the judging and awarding of the prizes it was not unusual for the company to arrange Sunday afternoon excursions so that the public could view the stations. The prizes awarded were small – the stationmaster of the winning station might have £5 to distribute amongst his staff. The scheme was phased out in the mid-sixties as more and more of the smaller stations were closed. As Bob

Ian S Carr

51. A2/1 Pacific 60507, 'Highland Chieftain', heads a northbound parcels train over Relly Mill viaduct on 6 January 1960. The A2/1 class, of which there were only four examples, was developed by Edward Thompson from the last four of the V2 2–6–2 class. The A2/1s and the A2/2s, the latter developed from Gresley's Ps 2–8–2 class, are considered to be amongst Thompson's least successful designs.

remarked, 'There's not much point in running a competition if there's only two entrants.' He did, however, have the satisfaction of seeing Holmfirth win first prize in 1965. He was quick to say that this was due to the efforts of the porter who was, according to Bob, a superb railwayman. He went on that when the porter retired the certificate awarding the first prize to Holmfirth was framed and presented to him. Until recently, occupying pride of place in the porter's house was that framed certificate.

'It must be remembered,' went on Bob, 'that in the early years of this century, the village station was the focal point of the community – hence the strong community feeling – and the stationmaster was a man of some standing.' He pointed out that in many instances the only telephone in the community was at the station; that people living in the village would come to the station to collect their newspapers and letters. It was not uncommon for the station staff to sell eggs – as a service and without the profit motive – and for the engine crews to ask for and to be supplied with chickens on request.

'I had a track walker at Moulton,' said Bob, 'who'd walked the branch for 38 years. He did a

69

52. A2/1 Pacific 60508, 'Duke of Rothesay', on a northbound Newcastle express train in 1959. This particular locomotive gained some notoriety when it was involved in a spectacular derailment at Southgate in July 1948. Bill Hoole was driving and fortunately he escaped with minor injuries, but his fireman, Albert Young, was knocked off the footplate by a length of rail and killed.

little bit today and so on and over a week he'd inspect the entire track. He was a marvellous naturalist and he always carried snares in his pocket. If you wanted a rabbit a word with old Bob was enough. He'd set his snares on the way up the branch and pick up his rabbits on the way back. The same with pheasants, I didn't know that a railway line could support so many pheasants.'

There were, at the time, six grades of station, grade six being the lowest. No doubt the quality of life at a grade five or six was very good, but if more salary was required then promotion had to be sought. But here a man could be caught between the devil and the deep blue sea. Up until nationalisation the railway company allowed stationmasters to act as agents for the supply of coal from a local colliery. Local people would buy the coal and pay the stationmaster. Then the system was changed and the stationmaster bought the coal from the colliery and sold it at a profit. There were some very good 'coal' stations on the LNER and Bob named Middleton in Teesdale and Bedale as examples. It is not difficult to appreciate the reluctance of a man to move from say a grade four station with a brisk coal trade to a grade three station without any coal concessions – quite obviously it could cost him money. On the other hand, when looking for promotion, a station with an engine shed attached was an attractive proposition because this brought an automatic increase in salary.

In Bob's case, his ultimate promotion in 1966 took him from Holmfirth and Clayton West to Newcastle upon Tyne as assistant stationmaster – assistant to the last tophatted stationmaster on BR.

The staff structure at Newcastle at that time

70

53. Darlington MPD on 26 March 1966 – the end of the steam era. A1 Pacific 60124, 'Kenilworth' (nameplates removed), is on main line pilot duty and waits patiently by the turntable whilst in the distance A1 Pacific 60145, 'St Mungo', in rather scruffy condition, adds to the general atmosphere of gloom and desolation.

was rather complex. The stationmaster who worked, nominally at least, from 09.00 – 17.00 hours had three assistants, one per shift. Below this top tier of management came the clerical grades looking after bookings, reservations and so on: then the platform staff, shunters, carriage and wagon staff and the guards. It is interesting to note that there were 131 passenger guards and one goods guard included in a staff of over 400 when Bob arrived at Newcastle. Whilst the stationmaster was responsible for train move-ments in the station he had no commercial responsibility, this was in the hands of the passenger agent and the parcels agent. An anomaly was that lost property and left luggage were dealt with by the parcels agent. The struc-ture was changed when the title of stationmaster was discontinued and the post of area manager was created. Parcels and passenger agents went into oblivion with stationmasters and, almost at a stroke, the area manager assumed responsi-bility for a staff of about 1,400 and an area covering North Tyne, South Tyne and as far west as Hexham. Initially, Durham remained a separate entity but eventually it too was swallowed up in the maw of the Newcastle area. The position of the assistant stationmasters was now ambiguous because there wasn't a stationmaster to assist! They became station assistants but there was some difficulty in defining precisely what this meant. Old habits die hard – perhaps nowhere as hard as on the railways and three years after the abolition of assistant stationmasters, staff were still referring to Bob and his two colleagues as ASMs. With commendable fortitude, higher management bowed to the inevitable. The title station assistant was abolished and assistant station manager was introduced. Thus, with the Englishman's penchant for compromise the time honoured initials, ASM, were officially re-introduced. Of course, no one mentioned the fact that there wasn't a station manager!

Receiving and attending to prominent people was very much part of the work at Newcastle. So far as Royal trains were concerned arrivals and departures were planned well in advance at board level and the stationmaster notified accordingly. In addition, each division and region through which the train would pass were advised. The necessary documentation was sent out and as Bob pointed out, once a procedure was established, then it became a routine matter. Invariably there was an engine change at Newcastle and operating and platform staff alike knew exactly where the train would stop. If any particular member or members of the Royal Family were to use the station as a station i.e. alighting from or joining a train, then due ceremony and protocol had to be observed. The Lord Lieutenant of the County was involved and there had to be liaison between his staff and BR management. Members of the welcoming party had to be in position in good time and something that became increasingly evident during Bob's time at Newcastle was that security had to be very tight. This was the joint responsibility of the civil and railway police forces, but even so the stationmaster was ultimately responsible for security within the station. He it was who must ensure that all entrances were locked and that extraneous items of railway paraphenalia such as luggage trolleys were either locked away or securely fastened – there must be no chance of anything falling onto the track or being thrown in front of or at the train. Bob provides us with a glimpse of the activity behind the scenes when the Queen went to Newcastle to open the Tyne Tunnel. Her itinerary was such that she used four stations in the area as stations – Her Majesty either left or joined the Royal Train four times in the course of the day. This stretched resources to the utmost, particularly as the division possessed only one red carpet.

'What actually happened,' said Bob, 'and these are the little things that people never see, the Queen alighted from the train at Newcastle and was greeted by the stationmaster – he is always the first person to greet the Queen off the train because it is his station. She was then greeted by the Lord Lieutenant who introduced remaining members of the official party to her. It was, of course, all arranged that the cars were waiting at a certain point and the Queen eventually departed. Immediately she left – and it was marvellous to see – a squad of men rolled up the carpet, all the plants and shrubs were removed and a lorry, that had been hidden out of sight around a corner, was whipped out onto the platform. Everything was loaded onto it, plants, shrubs, carpet and the barriers and immediately it was on its way to Jarrow, where the Queen was due to rejoin the train. The process then had to be repeated at Darlington and Stockton. Fortunately it all went swimmingly.'

If the Royal Train was only passing through,

H C Casserley

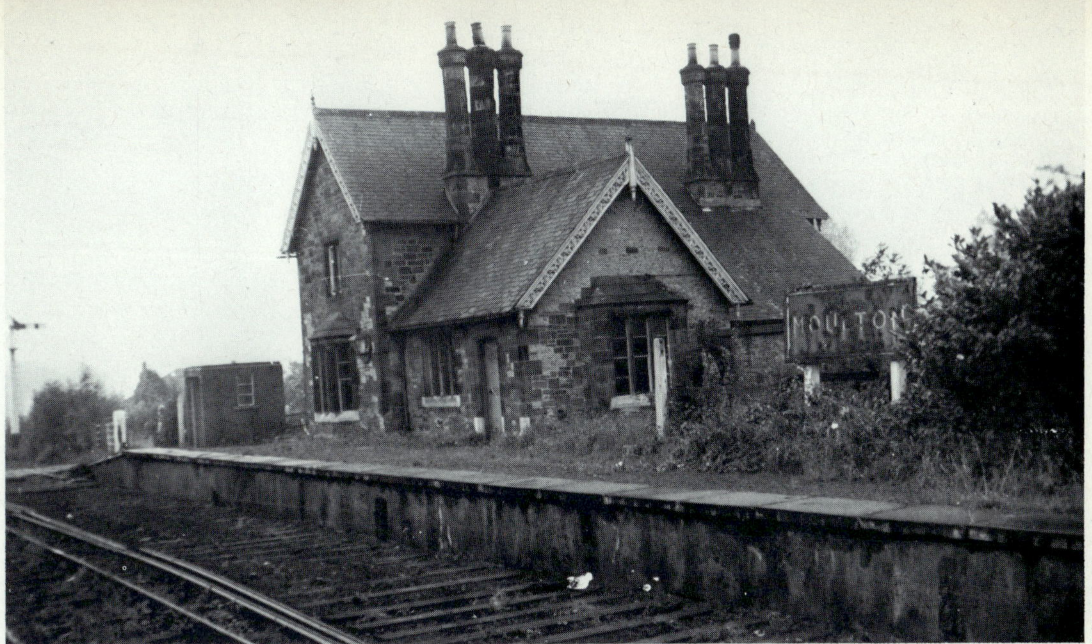

54. 'Ichabod, the glory is departed.' The remains of Moulton station on the Richmond branch as photographed in August 1971.

55. By October 1964 A3 Pacific 60062, 'Minoru', was mouldering on the scrap road at Gateshead MPD. The above photograph, taken only 15 months earlier, shows 60062 undergoing repairs in Doncaster works. Behind it is A3 Pacific 60106, 'Flying Fox'. This locomotive 'outlived' its companion by some two years, and towards the end of its days worked enthusiasts' specials.

D A Idle

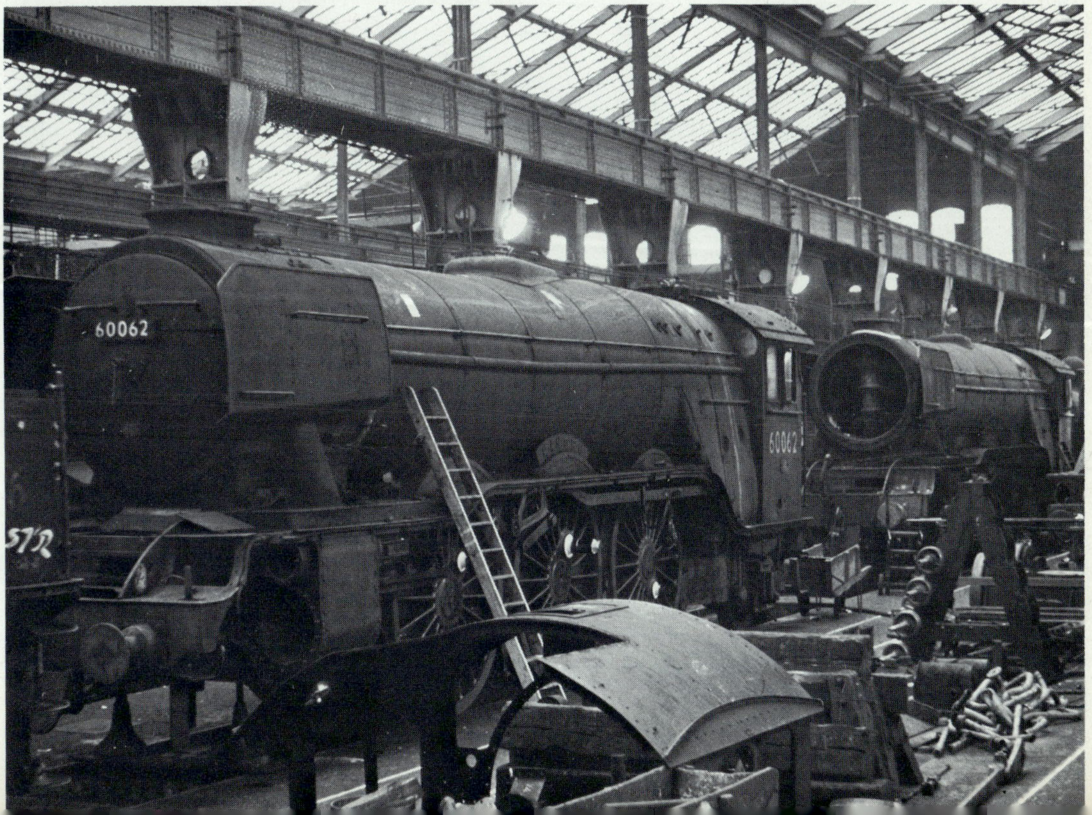

56. English Electric Deltic 9005, in original livery and un-named, whips up the snow just south of York with the up 'Tyne-Tees Pullman' on New Years Day 1962.

or stopping to change engines, security was just as stringent. The actual stopping time might be no more than ten minutes and it might be in the middle of the night, nevertheless the station-master was in attendance. Before leaving the subject of Royal Trains and prominent people, Bob said that his job had brought him into contact with the rich and famous from all walks of life. He was extremely reluctant to name drop but on being pressed he said that the most pleasant and considerate VIP that he had met was Dr A. M. Ramsey, former Archbishop of Canterbury. Very wisely Bob refused to name the most unpleasant but he did say, rather mysteriously, 'You'd be surprised.'

Turning from the ephemeral world of show-business, politics and crowned heads, Bob reflected, very philosophically, on the effects of nationalisation. There was, he averred, a lot of euphoria at the time although, in fact, very little happened for some considerable time. In essence the same people continued to run the railway and some of them probably still do. Eventually, the constituent companies' signs disappeared to be replaced by BR signs. This took sometime to work through but the changeover was far from dramatic. Staffing levels were unchanged and it was a while before the financial implications were felt. Just how much these were due to nationalisation or to the state of industry in

74

P H Wells

57. 'I tell you that's number two end.' Deltic 9019, 'Royal Highland Fusilier', awaits departure from King's Cross with an express for Newcastle on 12 April 1966.

general is a point of conjecture. Far more salutary were the effects of the war. When Bob returned from his service in the Navy he was struck by an overall 'tiredness'. Equipment was shoddy and didn't function quite as well as it should and it was not until after nationalisation when standardisation was introduced that things began to improve. Money was spent, capital was injected and eventually, he said, 'We all forgot that we'd worked for a private company.'

Discussing staff relationships Bob was of the opinion that as the system became truncated and the branch lines were closed, staff/management relations underwent a concomitant change. On the branch lines it was possible to know every member of the staff personally, but with the increase in the size of areas and divisions this was no longer possible. With a three shift system operating in a large centre, the railway became, in effect, three railways. There was a variation in approach to the job by the respective shifts and only a relief supervisor, who covered all shifts, had a perspective.

Changes in attitudes and in organisation brought changes in disciplinary procedures – drastic changes. Formerly, discipline was hard and fast – the offender was dealt with and that was the end of the matter. Now, the area manager instituted disciplinary action which was· then taken up by the appropriate department. It could become bogged down in the process so that it became meaningless. Bob was quick to point out, however, that discipline on the railway was still severe where potential loss of life was involved – drivers passing signals at danger was quoted as an example.

On the demise of steam, Bob was as positive as his colleagues in the footplate grades. 'It was,' he said, 'part of the development of the railways that has gone. To me, as an operating man, a steam engine, or any engine, was a unit of power

and I see no sentiment in it all. It's gone, it's finished with and we're on to something else.' He did concede, however, that the steam engine had the edge on the diesel so far as failures were concerned. He said that he could not remember more than two or three absolute failures during the steam days.

'About three years ago,' he said, 'I remember a Deltic failing in Newcastle Central. We had to get the pilot to move it and there was a 35 minute delay for the sake of a fuse – £250,000 of capital equipment rendered useless and the subsequent inconvenience it caused all for a 10p fuse. Admittedly, we had some poor running during the steam era but at least they kept going and could limp in; the engine might be down to 5 mph but it kept going and you could eventually get it out of the way at some convenient point.' He related an incident that happened during his days at Moulton which emphasised the previous statement. The last train from Darlington on Saturday night arrived at Moulton and the driver refused to go any further. As the stationmaster lived in the station house he was never off duty and was called out to deal with the recalcitrant driver, who, in turn, claimed that he was dealing with a recalcitrant engine. The fire had to be thrown out he said – the engine was not fit to move, not even one foot. Now there was a crossover at Moulton and the failed engine was standing on it. This meant that Bob would have to walk down the branch to Eryholme, to the main line, and instigate single line working procedures. He told the driver that he would have to wait with his engine until about 4.00 a.m. Miraculously, the driver found enough steam to move the engine and train off the crossing. But as Bob said, 'If that had been a diesel engine or a dmu, there it would have stood.'

Summarising his career and life, Bob Tait was guarded in answer to the time-honoured question, 'Would you do it all over again?' 'I've done exactly what I wanted to do. I knew that I would start at the bottom and I hoped that I'd get to King's Cross and the top hat. Well, I didn't quite make that – and in any case, by the time that I should have reached King's Cross, the top hat had gone – but at least I've done what I wanted to do and from that point of view I wouldn't change. Whether or not, in the light of experience and what has happened on and to the railways, I'd do it over again, I don't know. My father was a railwayman, I'm a railwayman but it stops here. I'm afraid that I wouldn't want my son to follow me – it's a different railway. They don't come to the railway as youngsters any more, they come as adults and in consequence they don't have the loyalty and it's not the same system. When I started, you knew what the system was and it was fair: you started at the bottom and worked up, now they start in the middle or at the top. But I've no regrets about my own life.'

7
Heirs of the LNER

In the wake of the 1955 Modernisation Plan, proposed and partially implemented by British Railways, came the withdrawal of steam locomotives and their replacement by diesel traction.

Being clever with the benefit of hindsight is a human failing and reflection on what might have been is not a particularly profitable exercise. Nevertheless, it is interesting to speculate what might have happened if those in authority had listened to that wayward genius of British steam, and an ex LNER man, O. V. S. Bulleid. He advocated the continuation of steam traction into the 1970s and then a change to electrification without intermediate dieselisation. In the light of events it seems that Bulleid has been totally vindicated, and it is a great pity that he was allowed to squander the final years of his working life designing peat-burning failures for CIE.

As it was, wholesale withdrawals and scrapping of the country's thousands of steam locomotives began in earnest in the late 50s and gathered momentum into the 60s.

The administrative heirs of the LNER – the Eastern, North Eastern and Scottish regions of BR – exercised caution in this respect and management appeared to adopt a logical policy. Whole classes of locomotives were not withdrawn overnight as was the case with the Western region Kings and the replacement of steam traction was done slowly and almost imperceptibly. In fact, intermediate overhauls of steam locomotives were being carried out at Darlington Works as late as the spring of 1965, alongside repairs to diesel locomotives.

A concomitant of the withdrawal of steam traction was the rise of the preservation movement. It seemed that the steam locomotive, vilified for years for being dirty and uneconomic, was suddenly imbued with an hitherto unrecognised glamour. There were a few precedents for this. The Stephenson Locomotive Society was active in preservation and restoration as long ago as 1927 and there were of course the collections at Swindon and at York, the latter consisting largely of former LNER locomotives. It is interesting to note that G. J. Churchward could not see any good reason why a broad gauge locomotive should be preserved following the conversion to standard gauge and, unfortunately, his able lieutenant, Stanier took this negative attitude with him when he was transferred to Euston.

Thus, preservation schemes mushroomed and the fact that we have so many preserved locomotives, both in private and in national hands, is due to the Herculean efforts of individuals and groups, whose labours have not always been helped and in some cases positively hindered by bureaucrats.

As already noted, withdrawals of former LNER locomotives appeared to be planned. The

58. A3 Pacific 4472, 'Flying Scotsman', approaches Kingswear on a very wet Friday in July 1973. The face peering somewhat furtively out of the fireman's window is that of the author's son, then aged nine. Shortly after arrival at Kingswear the author was sent into the tender to bring the coal forward and for this reason alone the weather is clearly remembered!

doubtful distinction of being the first Gresley Pacific to be withdrawn went to A3, 'Solario', in December 1959. The BRB had a sort of vague policy about scheduling certain locomotives for preservation. A4, 'Mallard', was, for obvious reasons, to be preserved and another A4 Pacific, 'Dwight D. Eisenhower', was destined for the U.S.A. From early 1960 withdrawals of former LNER Pacifics proceeded steadily as and when heavy general repairs, particularly boiler replacements, became necessary. Most of the locomotives went to Drapers of Hull for scrapping and, unlike Woodhams of Barry, Drapers lost no time in getting to work with the acetylene torch.

Towards the end of 1962, the name and number of A3 60103, 'Flying Scotsman', appeared on the withdrawals list and with what

seemed to be a piece of gross insensitivity those responsible could not, or would not, see any reason for preserving this locomotive which perhaps, more than any other, personified the spirit of the LNER. At this point, Alan Pegler stepped in, negotiated with Eastern Region and bought 'Flying Scotsman' out of service in January 1963. One or two other enthusiasts, no doubt spurred on by Alan Pegler's success, followed suit and A4s 60007, 'Sir Nigel Gresley', 60009, 'Union of South Africa', and 60019, 'Bittern', were subsequently purchased direct from BR.

The history of 'Flying Scotsman' since 1963 has been the subject of a range of articles. Its very existence and continued running is due to the efforts of a group of enthusiasts headed by George Hinchcliffe, general manager of Flying

59. The author preparing A3 Pacific 4472, 'Flying Scotsman', for its journey to Newport from Paignton, 12 September 1973.

Author's Collection

Scotsman Enterprises and financed by Bill McAlpine owner of the locomotive, who was responsible for rescuing it from the U.S.A. in 1973.

My contribution to the organisation has been modest but not, I hope, without some significance. I became involved with it in 1973 when 4472 – she reverted to her LNER number after restoration – spent 10 weeks working between Paignton and Kingswear on the Torbay Steam Railway. During that time I did whatever was required of me from showing visitors around the locomotive when on static display to spending one night on the footplate. The reason, for what was considered by my family and friends to be an act of masochism, was that 4472 was needed for publicity work very early in the

morning and she had to be kept in steam overnight, with someone to attend to the fire and to keep the boiler topped up. A volunteer was called for and I found myself on the footplate until I was relieved by George Hinchcliffe at about 3.30 a.m. It was an interesting experience and I must have done the job competently as the publicity programme went as planned. Furthermore, I was invited to take part, as a representative of Flying Scotsman Enterprises, in an exhibition at steam town Carnforth and one of the highlights of this was a trip from Kensington Olympia to Carnforth with 4472 and an exhibition train. The route planned for the journey was rather tortuous – it had to be to avoid running under overhead wires – and covered parts of the system formerly owned by three of the big four companies.

Apart from staff representing Flying Scotsman Enterprises there were volunteers from the Midland and Great Northern preservation group, who had undertaken to clean 4472 on arrival at Carnforth in return for the ride. We spent the day preparing the engine and coaxing the fire to burn without offending the smokeless sensitivities of the GLC and we were away from Olympia about three minutes late on a blustery Saturday evening and in the presence of a huge crowd.

During the course of the journey there were three changes of crew. The first set of men had travelled to Olympia 'on the cushions' and were to be relieved at Birmingham (Landor Street). They were not particularly enthusiastic about the job: for them it had come up on the roster and had to be done (I believe that union agreements now in operation have ensured that crews are rostered to steam workings only if they have not indicated otherwise). The driver handled

60. A3 Pacific 4472, 'Flying Scotsman', in Gateshead MPD on 29 June 1969 whilst working a railtour. Also in the picture is a representative selection of East Coast Main Line diesel motive power.

4472 well enough and the fireman was relieved of some of his work because one of the FSE volunteers, a former BR fireman, was resolved to fire up Hatton Bank where the line passes through the Forest of Arden and skirts the Clent Hills.

We ran easily enough from Olympia to Ealing and out through Denham, Gerrards Cross to Princes Risborough and on to Banbury where we stopped for water, aided and abetted by the local fire brigade. As we approached Leamington Spa, the volunteer fireman girded up his loins and went through the tenders. With Bill McAlpine at the regulator and the BR men offering advice he achieved his ambition and fired 4472 up Hatton Bank. I watched the proceedings with an air of detached interest resolving to fire the engine, should the oppor-

tunity present itself, only when she was running downhill with the regulator closed.

Once over Hatton I assisted the fireman through the clanking, swaying corridors in the tenders back to the compartment that we shared. Now I'd often heard the expression, 'a wet shirt', in relation to a fireman's efforts and on that occasion I actually assisted in peeling a wet shirt off a very wet back!

We stopped at Landor Street Junction and the crew that had brought us from Olympia was relieved by men from Leeds. I joined them on the footplate and, introductions over, I was told, rather curtly, to get into the fireman's seat and to keep out of the way. I'm not often taken aback but on this occasion I complied meekly and sat myself down.

'Hang on to that.' The request, if such it was,

came ·in a marked Leeds accent and a tape recorder was thrust into my hands. 'I've waited two years for this,' continued the fireman 'and nowt's going to get in my way.' Especially, was the implication, a ruddy volunteer. It transpired that both driver and fireman had volunteered for the job and had in fact been waiting for sometime for the opportunity to crew 4472. Although I was somewhat disappointed at being denied the privilege of swinging the shovel, I had at least a grandstand view of the proceedings.

We left Landor Street on time and I witnessed some spirited running between there and Burton. The driver perched on the edge of his seat and with his left arm on the window ledge and his right hand resting on the reverser he barely moved, apart from making adjustments to the cut-off, once he'd opened the regulator. The inspector accompanying us stood directly behind the driver and just occasionally they exchanged a word or two.

The fireman busied himself from the word go. He fired little and often and controlled combustion by deft adjustments to the flap on the firebox door. He kept the fire a very impressive whitish-yellow and as he opened the flap eerie shadows were cast around the cab, illuminating us but hardly penetrating the Stygian darkness outside.

As we approached Burton, adverse signals were sighted and we were 'turned inside'. We then ambled gently through Burton, rejoining the mainline. From then on frequent signal checks punctuated the remainder of the journey to Sheffield and the magic of the first part was never quite recaptured.

It was with evident reluctance that the crew handed 4472 over to another crew who were to take us over the final section from Leeds to Carnforth. Apart from Hatton Bank the journey had been over gently graded track, but the final section via Skipton, Hellifield and Long Preston would be testing to say the least. It was, therefore, with some misgivings that I noted, even in the dark, what seemed to be the extreme youth of the driver's mate. He climbed onto the footplate and viewed his surroundings in rather the same way that stout Cortez must have viewed the Pacific Ocean – 'Silent, upon a peak in Darien'.

So, with an inexperienced fireman it wasn't surprising that problems arose. On the climb to Hellifield the inspector had to rescue the fireman from his travails and to add to his burden the live steam injector began to give trouble. It was deemed necessary to summon assistance and Les Richards was hauled from his sleeping bag. His presence on the footplate brought an air of calm to a fraught situation; he cured the ailing injector and gave the kiss of life to the fire. Les went back to his compartment and the fireman back to his shovel, but it was to no avail and it was thanks to the driver and inspector that we limped into Carnforth. By the time that we arrived the fire was 'green' and the boiler pressure was falling steadily and what had been an eventful journey came to an end. Les re-appeared, worked his charms on the fire and it recovered sufficiently for us to do some shunting. As the overnight drizzle died away and dawn broke over the lakeside hills we unleashed the M & GN 'heavies' and they swarmed over 4472 like wasps round a jam pot.

The events that followed the run to Carnforth have been reported elsewhere. Suffice it to say that at the end of that Sunday there was an immaculate 4472 simmering gently in the afternoon sun watched over by a group of very tired but very contented heirs of the LNER.

Index